Eyes on Math

A Visual Approach to
Teaching Math Concepts

Eyes on Math

A Visual Approach to
Teaching Math Concepts

MARIAN SMALL

Illustrations by Amy Lin

Teachers College, Columbia University
New York and London

NATIONAL COUNCIL OF
TEACHERS OF MATHEMATICS

1906 Association Drive, Reston, VA 20191
www.nctm.org

NELSON EDUCATION

www.nelson.com

Published simultaneously by Teachers College Press, 1234 Amsterdam Avenue, New York, NY 10027, and National Council of Teachers of Mathematics, 1906 Association Drive, Reston, VA 20191; distributed in Canada by Nelson Education, 1120 Birchmount Road, Toronto, ON, Canada M1K 5G4.

Published by Teachers College Press, 1234 Amsterdam Avenue, New York, NY 10027

Library of Congress Cataloging-in-Publication Data

Small, Marian.
    Eyes on math : a visual approach to teaching math concepts / Marian Small ; illustrations by Amy Lin.
        pages   cm
    Includes bibliographical references and index.
    ISBN 978-0-8077-5391-0 (paper : acid-free paper)
        1. Mathematics—Study and teaching—Audio-visual aids.   2. Pictures in education.
    I. Lin, Amy.   II. Title.
    QA18.S63 2012
    510.71—dc23   2012030002

ISBN 978-0-8077-5391-0 (paper)
NCTM Stock Number: 14573

Printed on acid-free paper
Manufactured in the United States of America

20 19 18 17 16 15 14 13   8 7 6 5 4 3

Contents

Preface

A COLLEAGUE who works in the area of high school mathematics pointed out how well her students responded to the presentation of a simple picture that evoked mathematical thinking—no textbook or complicated activity was necessary. This got us thinking about the potential for a resource that focused on presentation of important mathematical ideas through pictures at all levels, not just for secondary grades.

ORGANIZATION OF THE BOOK

Chapter 1 provides an introduction that addresses some of the research on the value of visual representations of mathematical ideas. It also discusses the importance of questioning that evokes a deeper understanding of mathematical concepts.

Chapters 2, 3, and 4 provide visuals and questions for discussion of selected mathematical topics in grades K–2, 3–5, and 6–8, respectively. The intention is to help the teacher build a rich mathematical environment by using carefully constructed visuals to stimulate student thinking about mathematical concepts. Although, in certain instances, the visuals may seem similar to what educators have seen elsewhere, coupling the images with the carefully constructed questions that are provided is likely to be much more useful in developing robust understanding of the essential ideas underlying the concept the picture embodies than using either approach in isolation.

The online component of the book (available free at the Teachers College Press website: www.tcpress.com) provides vibrant color pictures that can form the basis of valuable mathematical conversations. These can be downloaded (as either PDF or JPEG files) and projected onto a classroom smart board or screen. The printed book provides teachers with support for these conversations by

- Clarifying the main idea that the visual is intended to bring out and specifying where that concept appears in the Common Core State Standards for mathematics. The Appendix provides a convenient listing of topics sorted by standard.
- Explaining why the idea is an important one to develop in a mathematics classroom
- Explaining how the particular mathematical idea relates to other mathematical learning
- Specifically explaining why the provided visual is likely to evoke the idea
- Providing a series of additional questions to use in a conversation with students about the picture and the underlying mathematical idea(s), along with an explanation for teachers about how each question develops a particular key understanding

- Providing extensions. These extensions challenge students to create a drawing, use manipulatives, or otherwise create a new and related example. The extensions can be used to help students reinforce the new learning, to help teachers assess understanding, or both.

USING THIS BOOK WITH OTHER RESOURCES

Most teachers will find that the activities in this book nicely supplement whatever textbook or other materials they currently use. Teachers might use the Appendix or table of contents to explore useful visuals based on the topic being taught. Many of the visuals and associated questions provided in this resource would make excellent introductory activities; others would make excellent consolidation activities. It is usually clear from the question on the visual or from the associated textual material whether the activity is more suitable before or after other instruction. In addition, the supporting material will help many teachers to decide where to focus their questioning on a concept and to recognize some of the important ideas they need to bring out.

USING THIS BOOK TO DIFFERENTIATE INSTRUCTION AND CONNECT GRADE TO GRADE

The nature of the activities provided will assist teachers attempting to differentiate instruction. The questions are often open enough to allow for rich conversations, whether students are struggling or are advanced. A number of the questions are suitable for different grade levels; the responses most likely will get more sophisticated as students move through the grades. Teachers will be able to see how to connect the mathematics in the grade they are teaching to content in lower and higher grades.

CREATING YOUR OWN VISUALS

The visuals and questions provided in this book may motivate you to create visuals and questions on your own. You can start with a mathematical concept you wish students to explore and then consider the important aspects of that concept that can be illustrated or suggested in a visual and explored further through questioning and class discussion.

For example, consider the notion that multiplying a number by 2 is the same as adding it to itself. Associated concepts that could be brought out include what multiplication means, what addition means, and the fact that the principle holds no matter what the number is that is being considered. The discussion could begin with a picture that shows 2 identical groups of 6 objects, 2 identical groups of 10 objects, and 2 identical bags that clearly hold a large, but unknown, number of small objects. The main question might be: Do these pictures show addition or multiplication? Supplementary questions could focus on what makes one say something shows multiplication or addition, and why it is not necessary to know how many objects are in the bags (assuming the bags are identical) in order to know whether the picture shows multiplication or addition.

Acknowledgments

FROM MARIAN SMALL

Without Amy Lin's amazing creative talent, this book could not have come to life. Her visuals make the book work.

I would also like to thank Jean Ward, our acquisitions editor at Teachers College Press, who was so understanding about our timelines and who has shown so much faith in our ability to produce something valuable for teachers and students.

FROM AMY LIN

I am forever asking questions—and learning all the time from my friend and coauthor Marian Small. I thank Marian and Jean Ward for giving me this opportunity to express my creative side.

I also thank my sister, Janice, for providing us with photographs. As always, I thank my family—Andrew, Jeremy, and Zachary—for their patience and support and for allowing me the time to work on this book.

Background

THIS BOOK IS FOUNDED on two bodies of research, one focusing on the vital role visualization plays in teaching and learning mathematics and one focusing on the importance of ensuring that students deeply understand the mathematical concepts with which they must deal.

VISUALIZATION IN MATH

When children are young, we use picture books not only to introduce them to the power of books and to the value and joy of being literate but also because visual images are powerful in helping us make sense of our world. Adams and Victor (1993) suggest that vision is the most important source of information about the world. Our embrace of the newest technologies, with the prominence of tablet computers and YouTube, indicates that we have become a highly visual culture in which pictorial images have begun to supplant the printed word as our preferred way of navigating the world.

Sadoski and Paivio (2001) have shown the critical role of visualization in the domain of reading, and it seems reasonable that the same would be true in the development of mathematical thinking.

Another researcher who has addressed the power of visual imagery is Edward R. Tufte (2001). Although he speaks primarily on the power of visual presentation of statistical data, his ideas can be easily generalized to other aspects of mathematical information.

Consider the power, for example, of showing why $3 \times 4 = 4 \times 3$ using the visual image below as compared with the more symbolic algebraic definition that appears on the next page.

A Visual Argument for Why $3 \times 4 = 4 \times 3$

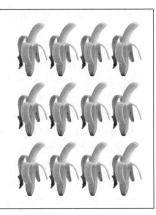

I see 3 rows of 4 bananas, but I also see 4 columns of 3 bananas.

Since $m \times n$ represents m groups of n items, I am seeing both 3×4 and 4×3 when I look at the same thing.

An Algebraic Argument for Why 3 × 4 = 4 × 3

$$3 \times 4 = 4 + 4 + 4$$
$$= 3 + 1 + 3 + 1 + 3 + 1$$
$$= 3 + 3 + 3 + (1 + 1 + 1)$$
$$= 3 + 3 + 3 + 3$$
$$= 4 \times 3$$

Similarly, consider the power of showing why the circumference of a circle is less than 4 times its diameter using the picture below, where the circumference of the circle is clearly less than the perimeter of the square, which has each side length equal to the circle's diameter.

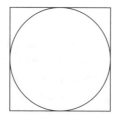

In fact, an interesting book at the secondary level is called *Proofs Without Words* (Nelsen, 2000). In its focus on higher level mathematical thinking, it shows how ideas are often more meaningfully demonstrated by using pictures as opposed to using symbols.

Rowan and Bourne (1994) have pointed out that understanding mathematical concepts is supported by children's ability to see how those concepts play out. This often involves the use of manipulatives, and it may be that it is not just the kinesthetic, but also the visual, aspect of using manipulatives that is what is relevant. Students can maintain visual images as they work through more abstract descriptions of ideas.

Murphy (2007) points out that it is "well thought-out and carefully developed visual/verbal co-expression of content" (p. 3) that is essential for visual learning.

FOCUSING ON THE IMPORTANT MATH

There has been an increasing emphasis on identifying "focal points" that should be addressed with students when teaching mathematics. This is evidenced in the *Curriculum Focal Points* series developed by the National Council of Teachers of Mathematics (2006), as well as the NCTM series *Developing Essential Understanding . . .* (e.g., Dougherty, Flores, Louis, Sophian, & Zbiek, 2010). The latter series helps teachers see the most important ideas in each of the topics addressed. Most recently, the effort to develop the Common Core State Standards for Mathematics (2010) has been an attempt to emulate high-performing countries where mathematics curricula appear to be more focused and more coherent than curricula used in the United States. The notion is that too many people view mathematics as a checklist of individual skills and concepts students must meet and master instead of seeing it as a connected web with a relatively small number of highly significant ideas that are visible in many individual situations.

At this point, the objective in developing methods for teaching mathematics is to focus not just on isolated topics but also on what it is about any topic that is important to emphasize. For example, Dougherty et al. (2010) list both big ideas and essential understandings for number and numeration for pre-K through grade 2. Rather than just suggesting how high students should count, or the size of the numbers they should add, these authors list concepts students should master in relation to number and numeration, including

- Recognizing that quantities can be compared without counting
- Recognizing that the size of a unit determines the number of times it must be iterated to count
- Recognizing that inherent in a place value system is the use of units of different size

Ideas such as these are addressed in the visuals and questions posed about them in the current book and the associated online materials.

BUILDING MATHEMATICAL COMMUNICATION

The National Council of Teachers of Mathematics (2000) has recognized the importance of communication in designating communication as one of the five mathematical processes it highlights. Connecting communication literacy to mathematics is also part of the Mathematical Practices of the Common Core State Standards. This emphasis is consistent with a body of research discussed by Lampert and Cobb (2003).

Building a math talk learning community is an integral step in improving mathematical understanding in a classroom. For the teacher, this involves a progression from simply asking factual short-answer questions to focusing on mathematical thinking and involving students as active participants in the development of concepts in the classroom.

Bruce (2007) points out that to cultivate valuable classroom communication, one of the important elements is the use of rich tasks. Hufferd-Ackles, Fuson, and Sherin (2004) suggest that a higher level of discourse is visible in a mathematics classroom when the teacher fosters an environment where students build on one another's explanations of ideas. Sullivan and Clarke (1992) discuss the importance of open-ended questions; they suggest the need for questions that require more than simple recall, that allow pupils to learn from the act of responding to the question, and that are open, with multiple possible correct answers. The questions associated with the visuals in this resource are such open and rich questions.

In the three chapters that follow, the value of visuals, the potential for high levels of communication, and a focus on important mathematical concepts will all be evident.

CHAPTER 2

Grades K–2

COUNTING UP BY 1s

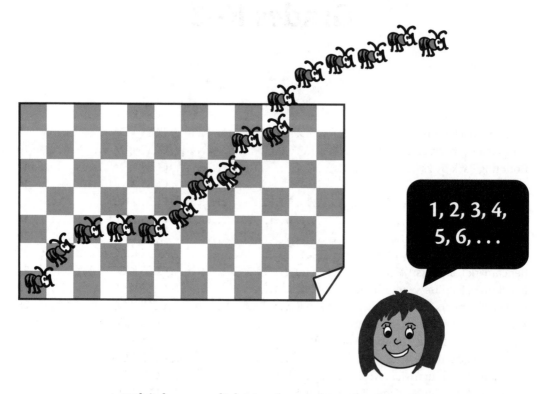

Which ants did Meghan already count?
How high will she go to count all of the ants?

◈ **IN THE EARLIEST GRADES**, counting is fundamental. Counting up by 1s is the first sort of counting students learn about. Students have many opportunities to count in real life and to count using counting books, but the focus should extend beyond the mechanics of counting. Students should be provided with opportunities to consider the *process* of counting.

Questioning students as they count should help them learn some of the fundamental principles of counting: that each number is counted once and only once, that we use a consistent set of number words (in any one language), that the last number spoken tells how many, that the order of objects counted is irrelevant, and that it makes sense to track what has already been counted and what has not. The concept of counting by 1s is first addressed in **Common Core State Standards K.CC**.

The picture provided here is designed to help students recognize that we want to find a way to distinguish what has already been counted from what must still be counted, and to give students an opportunity to see that we answer the question of how many there are by counting each item exactly once. It also provides the opportunity for students to use visual estimation: by looking at the ants off the blanket and comparing them to the ants on the blanket, students can see that there are more than 6 ants still on the blanket, so they will need to say more than 6 more numbers. This is a precursor to the notion that a number more than double 6 is more than 12.

❓ QUESTIONS to supplement the question with the picture and to include in a conversation about the picture include

- *Are you sure which 6 ants Meghan has already counted?* [We want students either to recognize the 6 ants off the blanket that Meghan might have already counted or to realize that Meghan could have counted any 6 of the ants.]

- *How do you know there are more than 6 ants still on the blanket?* [We want students to use visual skills to see that the number off the blanket is less than the number on the blanket.]

- *Which ant will you be touching or looking at when you say 10? 20?* [We want students to show their ability to count and, possibly, their recognition that the count can be done in different ways.]

- *If you had counted differently, would the number of ants be different?* [We want students to realize that a set can be counted in different ways, but the total does not change.]

- *What patterns do you notice when you count?* [We want students to notice patterns as they count, for example, that after 12, there is a set of "teen" numbers.]

◆ EXTENSION   Ask students to put out a fairly large set of objects and show two different ways to count how many there are.

COUNTING BACK BY 1s

36, 35, 34, 33, . . .

What numbers will be said next?
What does each of the numbers tell?

ALTHOUGH YOUNG STUDENTS are offered many opportunities to count up, there are fewer occasions when they are expected to count back. Yet not only is counting back practical for its own sake, it also supports later work in subtraction. Counting back is more difficult for students because they have to consider separately both how far back to count and how many are left. For example, to count back 3 from 10, you have to keep track of how many numbers you say, you have to realize that the number 10 is not counted, and you have to realize that the number left is not the 3 that you were thinking about.

Questioning about counting back should focus not only on how many are removed or how many are left but also on the process of counting. For example, students might notice the pattern of the numbers as they go down or they might notice that the numbers they say relate to what is left, but the *number* of numbers they say relates to the amount that has been removed. The concept of counting back by 1s is first addressed in **Common Core State Standards 1.OA**.

The picture provided here is designed to highlight the fact that if the first number you say as you are counting back is *thirty-six,* then originally there were 37, and not 36, items; we start counting back once an item has been removed. The picture also is designed to provide practice with counting back and to provide an opportunity to think about when we count back.

? **QUESTIONS** to supplement the question with the picture and to include in a conversation about the picture include

- *Why might someone count back?* [We want students to recognize that we count back when we are "getting rid" of things; the numbers we say tell how many items are left as one at a time is removed.]

- *What does the number of numbers you say tell?* [We want students to recognize that the number of numbers we say tells how many items are removed.]

- *How many cars were in the parking lot to start with? How do you know?* [We want students to realize that the number with which we begin is one more than the first number we say when we say a number each time an item is removed.]

- *If you continue counting back, will there be any numbers that have a **nine in them? Which ones?** [We want students to notice some of the patterns in the numbers as we count.]

- *Are there more items or fewer items left as you say more and more numbers as you count back?* [We want students to become aware that the more numbers we say, the fewer items are left.]

◆ **EXTENSION**   Ask students to count back by 1s from 45 and talk about how that is like counting back from 37 (as in the picture) and how it is different.

COUNTING UP BY 2s

What is the best way to count the bicycle wheels?

AT SOME POINT, students begin to learn how to count more quickly by using what is called "skip counting." Skip counting is only valuable if the "rhyme" of the skip counting words is familiar; for example, adults can skip count by 2, because we know the rhyme *2, 4, 6, 8, 10, . . .* without actually having to calculate anything. Adults are much less likely to skip count by, say, 6, because that rhyme is not as familiar.

Questioning about counting up by 2s should focus on situations in which skip counting by 2s makes sense, as well as on the numbers that we actually say. It is also important to consider the counting process, for example, that we skip count by 2s as long as we know the rhyme as far as we need it, that we probably skip count by 2s when it is easy to move or identify items two at a time, and that counting by 2s is always a choice. The concept of counting up by 2s is first addressed in **Common Core State Standards 1.OA**.

The picture provided here is designed to highlight the fact that sometimes it makes sense to both count by 1s and count by 2s to describe different aspects of a situation. Students, of course, also get the opportunity to practice counting by 2s.

❓ QUESTIONS to supplement the question with the picture and to include in a conversation about the picture include

- *Why is it a good idea to count by 2s when counting the wheels?* [We want students to recognize that when items come in 2s, they are relatively easy to count by 2s, and that it is quicker to count by 2s than by 1s.]

- *Would it make sense to count the bicycles (not the wheels) by 2s, or would you count them by 1s? Explain.* [We want students to realize that within the same situation you can choose, or not, to count different items in the same way.]

- *In what other situations would you count by 2s?* [We want students to generalize the bicycle wheel situation to other situations where items come in 2s.]

- *Suppose there were more than 100 items. Would you still count by 2s?* [We want students to realize that they can make choices about the way to count and that they might consider 2s not efficient enough sometimes.]

- *Could you always count up by 1s instead of by 2s if you wanted to?* [We want students to know that one can always count by 1s.]

- *You skip over some numbers when you count by 2s. For example, you never say 1, 3, 5, ... Why is it okay to skip those numbers?* [We want students to realize that we are still counting everything when we skip count by 2s, since the number we do not say is associated with the first item in the set of two being counted.]

◆ EXTENSION   Ask students to describe or draw a situation where they think they might consider counting by 2s and one where they would not, and to talk about why.

COUNTING BACK BY 2s

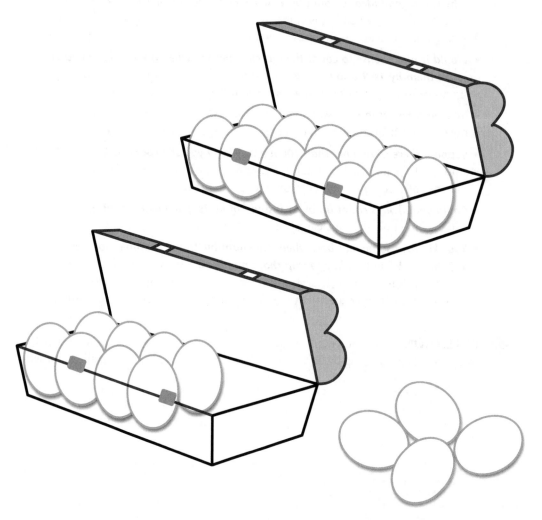

Mom is counting how many eggs are left each time she takes some out. What numbers will she say if she takes out 2 eggs at a time?

❖ **JUST AS STUDENTS NEED** to consider what is involved in counting back by 1s, we also want them to experience what is involved in counting back by 2s. Again, students must realize the type of situation in which this makes sense—likely one where items come in 2s or can easily be grouped in 2s, where items are being removed from a known total, and where we are interested in how many are left.

Questioning about counting back by 2s should focus on the kinds of situations in which this makes sense, as well as on the numbers that we actually say. It is important to consider the counting process, for example, that we are more likely to skip count back by 2s when we know the counting-by-2s rhyme in both directions. We also want students to know that counting back by 2s is always a choice. The concept of counting back by 2s is first addressed in **Common Core State Standards 1.OA**.

The picture provided here is designed to highlight the facts that, as we count back by 2s, there are numbers that are skipped and the numbers that we say decrease. The picture also shows a situation where items are easily visualized in pairs.

? QUESTIONS to supplement the question with the picture and to include in a conversation about the picture include

- *How is counting back by 2s like counting up by 2s? How is it different?* [We want students to realize that the same numbers are said when counting up or counting back; only the order changes.]

- *Why might you count back by 2s instead of counting back by 1s to count the number of eggs left?* [We want students to recognize the efficiency of counting back by 2s when items come in 2s.]

- *Why would you not count back by 2s if you didn't know how many to start with?* [We want students to realize that we only count back when we know how many there were to start with.]

- *What do the numbers you say when you count back by 2s tell you?* [We want students to recognize that the numbers you say indicate how many are left, and not how many are removed.]

- *If Mom said 22, 20, 18, 16, how many eggs would she have removed from the cartons? How do you know?* [We want students to realize that you use the number of numbers you say to help figure out how many were removed; in this case, Mom would have removed 4 sets of 2, or 8, eggs.]

- *In what other situations would you count back by 2s?* [We want students to generalize the egg situation to other situations where items are removed in 2s from a known total.]

- *Could you always count back by 1s instead of by 2s if you wanted to?* [We want students to know that one can always count back by 1s.]

◆ EXTENSION   Provide an odd number of counters, for example, 25 of them. Tell students there are 25. Ask them to count back by 2s. Ask what happens and why.

COUNTING UP BY 5s

Count to know how much money Keesha has.

❖ **AS STUDENTS WORK** with larger numbers, they benefit by learning more efficient ways to count. One comfortable way for many students to count larger quantities is counting by 5s, since it seems to be relatively easy to learn the counting-by-5 rhyme.

Questioning about counting up by 5s should focus on situations in which this makes sense, as well as on the numbers that we actually say. For example, counting by 5s makes sense when counting nickels, tally marks, the value of a pile of $5 bills, the number of fingers on hands, or the number of toes on feet—all items that are organized in 5s. It is also important to consider the counting process, for example, that we skip count by 5s when there is a fairly large number of items and when it is easy to move or identify items five at a time. Students can also consider how quickly numbers grow as they count by 5s as compared to counting by 2s or 1s. The concept of counting up by 5s is first addressed in **Common Core State Standards 2.NBT**.

The picture provided here is designed to make it possible to consider the fact that as we count the value of the money we might count by 5s, but we probably do not count by 5s to count the number of nickels.

? **QUESTIONS** to supplement the question with the picture and to include in a conversation about the picture include

- *What do the numbers 5, 10 represent in the picture?* [We want students to realize that the 5, 10 could represent the value of the two coins that are moved to the side.]

- *When do you say words that include* five *when you count by 5s? When don't you?* [We want students to notice the patterns in counting by 5; every second word (other than *fifteen*) has the word *five* at its end.]

- *Do you ever say words that end with* two*? Why not?* [We want students to realize that many numbers are not said when counting by 5s.]

- *What other sorts of numbers, other than those that end in* five*, do you say?* [We want students to recognize that the numbers we say are multiples of 10 (e.g., *twenty, thirty, forty*), unless the word for the number ends in *five* (except for *fifteen*).]

- *How would you count the number of coins (not their value)? Why that way?* [We want students to recognize that different elements in the same situation might be counted differently.]

- *Why wouldn't you count the value of the coins by 2s?* [We want students to realize that if items naturally come in 5s, it would be awkward to count them by 2s.]

- *Compare how high you get when you count by 5s three times to how high you get when you count by 2s three times. Why does that happen?* [We want students to observe that when you count by a higher number, you increase faster.]

- *Are there any numbers you say when you count by 5s that you also say when you count by 2s?* [It can help students to notice that there is overlap between the numbers said when counting in different ways. It reminds them there is more than one way to count.]

◆ **EXTENSION**   Tell students that Ethan counted some items by 5s. He said there were still some items left to count but not enough to say another number. Ask them to tell how many items there might have been.

COUNTING BACK BY 5s

Andrew is buying candies. How much money will he have left after he buys each candy?

⬙ **STUDENTS NEED TO RECOGNIZE** that when we count back—whether by 1s, 2s, or 5s—items are being removed from a known total and we are interested in how many are left. But we are likely to count back by 5s, rather than 1s or 2s, when the items come in 5s, when the rhyme for counting by 5s is familiar, and when there are many items.

Questioning about counting back by 5s can involve actually doing the counting, but should also focus on the counting process. The concept of counting back by 5s is first addressed in **Common Core State Standards 2.NBT**.

The picture provided here is designed to highlight the fact that the numbers we say as we count back by 5s tell us how much is left after one or more 5s are removed.

QUESTIONS to supplement the question with the picture and to include in a conversation about the picture include

- *Why is figuring out how much money is left after you buy each candy the same as counting back by 5s?* [We want students to relate counting back by 5s to situations that would encourage us to do that.]

- *How is counting back by 5s like counting back by 2s? How is it different?* [We want students to realize that counting back by anything involves starting with a total and gradually removing the same amount over and over.]

- *Why might you count back by 5s instead of by 2s to count the amount of money left?* [We want students to recognize the efficiency of counting back by 5s when items come in 5s.]

- *What will be the last few numbers you say? How do you know?* [We want students to realize that when you count back by 5s, the last numbers you will are say 10, 5, 0.]

- *How do you know how many numbers Andrew would say before he uses all his money?* [We want students to distinguish between how many numbers are said and the actual money values those numbers represent.]

EXTENSION   Ask students to think about how counting back by 5s could have helped if Andrew had had 3 quarters instead of 12 nickels.

COUNTING UP BY 10s

Count the number of fingers,
one set of handprints at a time.

❖ **COUNTING UP** by 10s is a critical skill to ready students for working with the place value system. It also can help them to estimate numbers and to count large groups.

Questioning about counting up by 10s should focus on situations in which this makes sense, as well as on the numbers that we actually say. For example, counting by 10s makes sense when counting dimes, sets of fingers or toes, the value of a pile of ten-dollar bills, or the value of a set of base ten rods, all of which are organized in 10s. It is also important to consider the counting process, for example, that we skip count up by 10s when there are many items and when it is easy to move or identify items ten at a time. Students can also consider how quickly numbers grow as they count by 10s, compared to counting by 2s or 5s. By the time students are skip counting by 5s and

10s, they might also be considering what to do when the number is not an exact number of tens (or fives). For example, if there were 82 items, one might count 10, 20, 30, 40, 50, 60, 70, 80, and then switch to 81, 82. The concept of counting up by 10s is first addressed in **Common Core State Standards 2.NBT**.

The picture provided here is designed to highlight the fact that as we count the groups of fingers we might count by 10s, but we probably would not count by 10s to count the number of children whose hands are shown.

❓ QUESTIONS to supplement the question with the picture and to include in a conversation about the picture include

- *Why does the count go so fast? You got all the way to 80 and did not say many numbers.* [We want students to realize that if you count many items at a time, as is required by counting the fingers one person at a time, the count goes quickly.]

- *What if the last child had only printed one of his hands? Would you count by 10s the whole time or just most of the time? Explain.* [We want students to recognize that you can only count by 10s exclusively if the total is a multiple of ten. Otherwise a combination of counting by 10s and counting in some other way is required.]

- *When would you count by 10s and when wouldn't you?* [We want students to recognize that we count by 10s when items come in groups of 10.]

- *How would your count have been different if you had counted one hand at a time, instead of one person at a time?* [We want students to recognize that if you can count by 10s, you can also count by 5s, but the count is slower.]

◆ EXTENSION Provide students with a loose set of 50–100 linking cubes. Suggest that they make as many stacks of 10 as possible. Ask why it is easier to count the cubes after stacking than before.

COUNTING BACK BY 10s

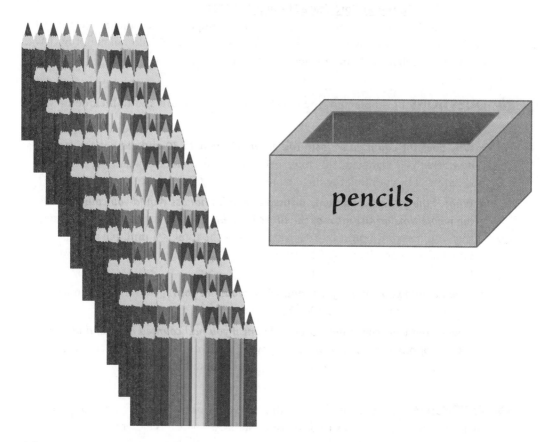

There are 100 pencils. You put the pencils from one row at a time into the box. Count to tell how many pencils are left outside of the box each time that one row of pencils is removed.

❖ **AS IN OTHER COUNTING BACK SITUATIONS**, students need to recognize that we count back when items are being removed from a known total and we are interested in how many are left. But we are likely to count back by 10s when the values are reasonably high and when items are easily grouped in tens.

Questioning about counting back by 10s can involve actually doing the counting but should also focus on the counting process. The concept of counting back by 10s is first addressed in **Common Core State Standards 2.NBT**.

The picture provided here is designed to highlight the fact that the numbers we say as we count back by 10s tell us how many items are left after one or more groups of 10 are removed.

? **QUESTIONS** to supplement the question with the picture and to include in a conversation about the picture include

- *Why is it helpful to know that there were 100 pencils to start with?* [We want students to realize that one cannot count back without knowing the total.]
- *What is the first number you say as one row of pencils is put into the box?* [We want students to realize you say 90, not 100, as the first row of pencils is removed from the others.]
- *How is counting back by 10s like counting back by 5s? How is it different?* [We want students to realize that counting back by anything involves starting with a total and gradually removing the same amount over and over.]
- *What other numbers might be easy to count back by as pencils are put into the box?* [We want students to notice that in this case counting back by 5s or even by 2s might be reasonable.]
- *When would someone counting back by 10s to count the number of pencils left outside the box say the number 10?* [We want students to recognize that this would be when one full row remains, since that would indicate that 10 pencils remain.]
- *Suppose you counted back by 10s starting at 82. What do you notice about the numbers you would say?* [We want students to recognize that the ones digit never changes in this situation.]

EXTENSION   Ask students to think about how counting back by 10s can help them subtract 30 on a 100-chart.

COMPARING NUMBERS BY MATCHING

The buttons at the top are arranged into two lines in two different ways. Which way makes it easier to tell which line has more buttons?

INITIALLY, STUDENTS LEARN to compare numbers by matching them, one to one (1-1), to see which set has "leftovers." Eventually students learn to compare by just comparing the numbers describing the size of the sets, but it is important for students to understand why 1-1 correspondence is a useful way to compare. Later, in more complex mathematics, this can still be a valuable skill.

Questioning about 1-1 correspondence should focus on the fact that the items need not be identical, but they must be matched so that it is visually easy to see which group has more; usually that requires matching almost as if the items were in a grid. Another important idea to bring out is that the definition of *being more* is that there are items without matches once items in one of the sets have been matched 1-1 with items in the other set. The concept of comparing using 1-1 correspondence is first addressed in **Common Core State Standards K.CC**.

The picture provided here is designed to highlight the fact that the items need not be identical but that they can still be matched 1-1. Students might notice that even though the same set of buttons is used in the left pair as in the right pair, the second set of the right pair (the one on the far right) is spread out differently. Many students will choose the left pair, but some students might notice that the right pair matches three buttons in the left line to two in the right line and feel that this is an easy comparison too.

? **QUESTIONS** to supplement the question with the picture and to include in a conversation about the picture include

- *Is it useful to line up the items to decide which set has more?* [We want students to understand that lining up allows us to get a better sense of the size of a group than we would get otherwise.]

- *How did you decide that this (the teacher points to the group on the left in the first pair) line had more buttons than the other?* [We want students to articulate that when items are matched, all you have to do is notice that there are "extras" with no match.]

- *How did you decide that this (the teacher points to the group on the left in the second pair) line had more buttons than the other?* [We want to find out if students create their own sort of 1-1 matching, for example, matching some buttons on the right with one on the left and some with two on the left, recognizing that this means there are fewer on the right.]

- *What would be another way to compare whether one set of buttons has more than another?* [We want students to realize that you can compare sizes by using numbers. The number that is said later in the counting sequence denotes the larger set.]

◆ **EXTENSION**   Ask students to use buttons or counters to create two sets and arrange them so that one set has more than the other but does not look that way.

BENCHMARK NUMBERS: ALL ABOUT 5

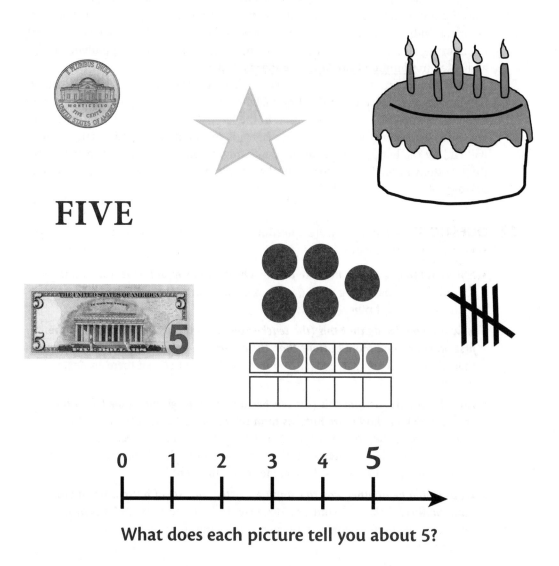

What does each picture tell you about 5?

◈ **WE OFTEN HAVE STUDENTS** represent a number in many ways, but it is when they focus on how each representation shows something different about the number that they gain a deeper understanding of that number. Five is an important benchmark number for young students. They relate many of the first numbers they learn to how many more or less than 5 those numbers are.

Questioning about representations of 5 should bring out properties of 5. For example, students might think of how 5 compares in size to other numbers, like 10, whether it is odd or even, the fact that it is 1 more than double 2, the fact that it is

1 less than double 3, etc. The use of 5 as a benchmark number is suggested in **Common Core State Standards K.CC**.

The picture provided here is designed to make sure students realize that different representations of 5 tell different things about it, for example, that 5 comes after 1, 2, 3, 4 when the counting sequence is used, that 5 can be modeled as a single item, like a nickel, that it is used to tally, that it is half of 10, that is it 1 more than double 2, etc.

? **QUESTIONS** to supplement the question with the picture and to include in a conversation about the picture include

- *Which pictures are most alike?* [We want students to analyze how different representations of a number show different things about it. For example, students might think of the number line and the tally marks as most alike since they both have four items of one type and the fifth is special. These both show 5 as 4 and 1.]

- *Which picture makes it really easy to see that 5 is less than 10?* [We want students to observe that it is pictures that simultaneously show 5 and 10, like the 10-frame, that make it easiest to compare 5 to 10.]

- *Which picture makes it really easy to see that 5 is not an even number?* [We want students to recognize that a number is even if items are matched up in pairs. The picture showing 5 as 2 sets of 2 and 1 more shows most easily that 5 is not even.]

- *Which picture makes it really easy to see that 5 is more than 4?* [We want students to recognize that pictures that simultaneously show 4 and 5 (so not a nickel, and not the word *five*), make it easiest to compare 4 to 5.]

◈ **EXTENSION**   Ask students to represent 5 in other ways and to explain what each way tells about 5.

BENCHMARK NUMBERS: ALL ABOUT 10

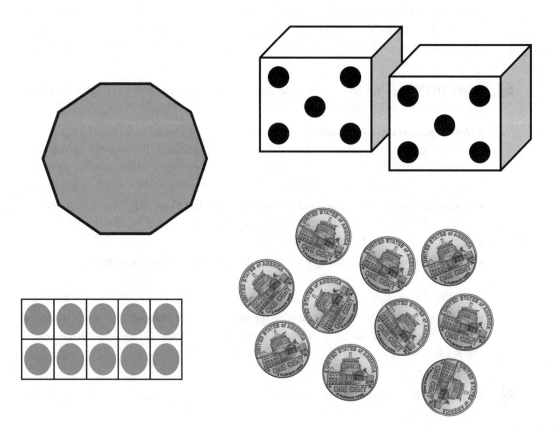

What do all of the pictures have in common?

❖ **THE NUMBER 10** is fundamental to students' growing understanding of mathematical ideas. The number 10 serves as a benchmark to which other numbers are compared, but it is also the basis for our entire place value system, whether working with whole numbers or decimals.

Questioning about representations of 10 should bring out its properties. For example, students might think of how 10 is double 5 or how 10 is an even number. The use of 10 as a benchmark number is suggested in **Common Core State Standards K.CC**.

The picture provided here is designed to make sure students recognize that there are many representations for this very important number. In most of the cases here, the "ten-ness" is obvious, but in one, the fact that there is ten of something (the ten sides of the shape) is more subtle.

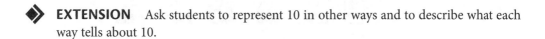 **QUESTIONS** to supplement the question with the picture and to include in a conversation about the picture include

- *Which pictures show you that 10 is two 5s?* [We want students to recognize that several of the pictures show this. For example, the picture of the dice and the 10-frame both show 10 as two identical sets of 5.]

- *Which pictures make it harder to see about how much 10 actually is?* [We want students to see that pictures that do not explicitly show 10 as 10 individual items make it harder to see how much 10 really is.]

- *What picture of 10 could you draw to show that 10 is more than 8?* [We want students to think of possibilities for representing 10 and 8 in the same picture that make it easy to see that the 8 is less than 10. One possibility is to use a number line, another is to use a 10-frame (removing 2 counters for 8), and yet another possibility is to use 1-1 correspondence.]

- *What picture could you draw to make it easy to see that 10 is less than 20?* [Some possibilities are showing a 10-rod and two 10-rods; showing two full 10-frames and comparing them to one full 10-frame; or showing a line of 10 items, each of which is matched to one of the 20 items on another line.]

- *How could you use the pictures of 10 to easily create pictures of 9?* [We want students to view 10 as a benchmark, recognizing that 9 can be thought of as 1 less than 10.]

EXTENSION   Ask students to represent 10 in other ways and to describe what each way tells about 10.

ORDINAL NUMBERS

Which elephant is fourth?

❖ **ALTHOUGH WE TEND TO FOCUS** on the counting, or cardinal, numbers in school mathematics, we also use ordinal numbers—numbers that relate quantity to position—both in everyday life and in school. For example, we might ask who is first in line, which shape is the tenth one in the pattern below, or what the eighth number is in a skip counting pattern such as 10, 20, 30, ...

We want students to understand that each ordinal number, such as *fifth,* is related to a cardinal number, in this case *five.* Additional questioning about ordinal numbers should not only focus on their relationship to the cardinal numbers but also on another very important idea—that ordinal numbers depend on perspective. When we count using cardinal numbers, a set of 6 is 6, no matter how we count it. But if we look at a line of dots from different perspectives, the sixth dot from one perspective (e.g., from the left) might be the fifth from another perspective (the right).

It is also useful to familiarize students with the language of ordinal numbers (e.g., *fifth, sixth, seventh*) before they begin working with fractions. Although ordinality is not explicitly mentioned, it is implicit in **Common Core State Standards K.CC**, because using ordinal numbers provides meaningful opportunities for students to practice counting.

The picture provided here is designed to focus students on both issues associated with ordinal numbers—their relationship to cardinal numbers (*fourth* relates to the number *four*) and the issue of perspective.

? **QUESTIONS** to supplement the question with the picture and to include in a conversation about the picture include

- *What does being fourth have to do with four?* [We want students to notice how the word *four* appears in the term *fourth* and why.]
- *Where is the second elephant? What makes it second?* [We want students to recognize that the term *second* relates to *two,* even though the words do not sound alike.]
- *Is there a name for every position in the line?* [We want students to realize that every object in a group has an ordinal name (or even more than one).]
- *If you look at the line a different way, could the fourth elephant become the seventh elephant?* [We want students to recognize that naming an item with an ordinal designation requires choosing a position that will be designated first and recognizing that this choice could be viewed as arbitrary.]

◆》 **EXTENSION**   Ask students to draw a picture of shapes in which a square could be viewed as either third or ninth, depending on your position when you look.

ADDITION AS COMBINING

What different addition sentences might tell how many books will be on each shelf after putting away the books on the floor?

❖ **THE FIRST MATHEMATICAL OPERATION** students are exposed to is usually addition. They learn that we use addition when certain items join other items. These joining situations initially involve counting, but the process can eventually be short-cut, once addition facts are known, to avoid the requirement of counting.

Questioning about addition as combining should focus on what the numbers in the addition sentence represent, the fact that the total (or sum) is greater than either number being added (the addends) if more than 0 is added, and the notion that the total can be determined by adding on to any of the addends. The concept of addition as combining is first addressed in **Common Core State Standards K.OA**.

The picture provided here allows for conversation about a variety of number sentences. If all 6 books were added to one shelf, sentences such as 3 + 6 = 9, 5 + 6 = 11, or 7 + 6 = 13 could be discussed. If the additional books were split among shelves, sentences such as 3 + 2 = 5 and 7 + 4 = 11 could be discussed. There are many other possibilities.

? QUESTIONS to supplement the question with the picture and to include in a conversation about the picture include

- *What does each number in your number sentences represent?* [We want students to recognize the meaning of each addend and the sum.]

- *Why do you know there will be no totals less than 3?* [We want students to realize that a sum must be at least as great as the addends, when the addends describe objects that can be counted.]

- *What might the greatest total be? How do you know?* [We want students to practice combining some numbers.]

- *To figure out what 3 + 4 is, why can you say 5, 6, 7?* [We want students to realize that you can count on from one of the values to determine a total.]

- *Why is it possible to write many different sentences for this situation?* [We want students to realize that the structure of the problem allows for many possibilities.]

◆ EXTENSION   Ask students to draw two different pictures that show what 6 + 3 might represent.

ADDITION TO DESCRIBE
PART-PART-WHOLE SITUATIONS

What does each picture show about addition?

ALTHOUGH WE OFTEN ASSOCIATE addition with an active "joining" situation—where some items join other items—addition is also used to describe parts of a whole. For example, in a household with 2 males and 4 females, the sentence 2 + 4 = 6 tells how the two parts make a whole, the number of people in the household. The difference between this situation and a joining situation is that in this case one does not have the sense that there was a starting point and then more joined. In this case, there are just two pieces.

Questioning about adding to describe part-part-whole situations should focus on the relationship between these situations and joining situations and on what the parts of number sentences describing the situations mean. It is also important to recognize that we add to avoid the need to count large quantities. The concept of addition as describing part-part-whole situations is first addressed in **Common Core State Standards 1.OA**.

The picture provided here offers an opportunity to focus on adding as a way to avoid counting while also focusing on part-part-whole situations. In each case, there are two clearly identifiable subgroups of cupcakes.

? QUESTIONS to supplement the question with the picture and to include in a conversation about the picture include

- *How is counting the number of cupcakes in each picture like figuring out how many cupcakes there would be if we started only with the cupcakes with cherries and then someone else brought over the other ones?* [We want students to relate the two different meanings of addition.]

- *Why might you figure out the number of cupcakes in the last picture by saying 19, 20?* [We want students to relate part-part-whole situations to counting on.]

- *How could you figure out how many cupcakes there are in the second picture without counting each of them?* [We want students to realize either that they can count on from one of the amounts (either 16 or 4) or that they can use what they know about addition.]

- *Why is it easy to tell that if there are more cupcakes with cherries, then there are fewer without cherries?* [We want students to realize that when the total is the same, if one part is smaller, then the other part is larger.]

◆ EXTENSION   Ask students to draw a picture that shows a whole group of 10 made up of two parts, and ask what the addition sentence describing the picture would be.

ADDING 0 AND ADDING 1

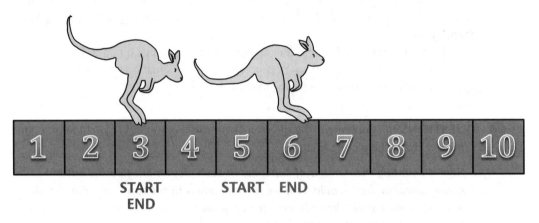

START   START END
END

The kangaroos started at 3 and 5.
The picture shows where they landed after one jump.
What number sentences tell about each kangaroo's jump?

AS STUDENTS APPLY the meaning of addition to various situations and try to learn strategies to minimize the number of separate facts they must remember, they encounter the idea that there are generalizations related to adding 0 or adding 1 that allow them to learn two rules instead of 20 individual facts. They find out that adding 0 results in no change to a number and adding 1 produces the next counting number.

Questioning about adding 0 and adding 1 should focus on *why* the generalizations are what they are, not just on memorizing the rules. In particular, students should see how the principles of counting explain the rules. When we count, if there is one additional item, we say the next number, so adding 1 results in the next number. When there are no additional items, there are no more numbers to say in the count, so the last number said (the original amount) is unchanged. These types of addition strategies are first addressed in **Common Core State Standards 1.OA**.

Using a number line is one of the best ways to make sense of the generalizations involved in adding 0 or adding 1. The picture provided here helps students to see that if you jump in place, it is like adding 0, and you end up where you started. But if you jump 1, you land at the next value, or add 1.

QUESTIONS to supplement the question with the picture and to include in a conversation about the picture include

- *Why is it easy to add 0?* [We want students to see that adding 0 does not really involve knowing anything other than where you started.]

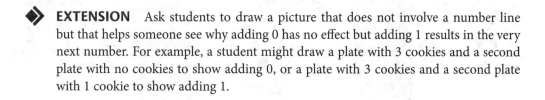

- *Why is it hard to show a picture of adding 0?* [We want students to think of the practical difficulty of showing nothing, recognizing that zero is really an abstraction.]

- *Why is it easy to add 1?* [We want students to realize that adding 1 merely involves saying the next number, because when we count, we say one more number to add the one extra item.]

- *If a kangaroo started at a different place, would adding 0 have the same effect?* [We want students to generalize the principle to any situation.]

- *If a kangaroo started at a different place, would adding 1 have the same effect?*

◆◆ **EXTENSION**   Ask students to draw a picture that does not involve a number line but that helps someone see why adding 0 has no effect but adding 1 results in the very next number. For example, a student might draw a plate with 3 cookies and a second plate with no cookies to show adding 0, or a plate with 3 cookies and a second plate with 1 cookie to show adding 1.

ADDITION: COMMUTATIVITY

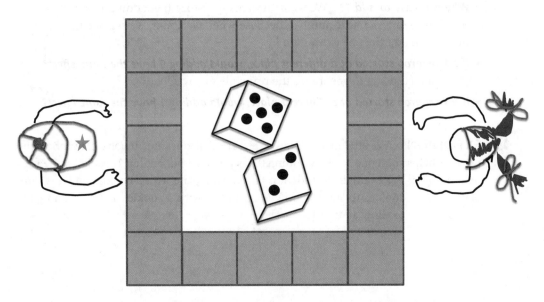

Why might Amy and Aaron write different number sentences to tell what the dice roll is?

THERE ARE MANY PRINCIPLES that describe addition, subtraction, multiplication, and division that simplify the number of individual pieces of information that must be committed to memory. One of these principles is that the order of adding two numbers is irrelevant; the sum is the same if the order is switched. This is formally called the commutative property of addition. The same is not true of subtraction, so it is important that students develop a sense of why the commutative property is true for the particular operation of addition.

Questioning about commutativity of addition should focus on why the property holds. Fundamentally, it is because addition involves combining, and items can be combined and then counted in any order. This property is first addressed in **Common Core State Standards 1.OA**.

Rather than simply calculating a lot of examples and observing that 4 + 3 turns out to be the same as 3 + 4, that 5 + 8 turns out to be 8 + 5, etc., the picture provided here demonstrates why the answers have to be the same. Without an understanding of why, students could have no assurance that just because the order of addition does not matter sometimes, it might not matter at other times. The picture shows that when two amounts are combined, you can look left to right or right to left; the total number of objects cannot be different, but the sentences written might well be.

? **QUESTIONS** to supplement the question with the picture and to include in a conversation about the picture include

- *Suppose there were special dice that showed 4 and 9. What number sentence would Amy write? Why? Do you think Aaron would write the same sentence?* [We want students to write their own number sentence for an addition situation and then entertain the possibility that, based on point of view, the two children could write different number sentences describing the same situation.]

- *If Amy and Aaron wrote different sentences, what do you think would be the same about them?* [We want students to recognize that the sum would have to be the same, as would the two addends.]

- *Suppose the dice showed two even numbers that were different. What sentence might Amy write? What would Aaron write?* [We want students to relate number sentences to a situation, but because we want to develop a generalized understanding, a condition, rather than specific numbers, is provided.]

- *Why might it be useful to know that 2 + 9 = 9 + 2?* [We want students to realize the value of knowing the commutative property—if one fact is known, another is automatically known.]

◆ **EXTENSION**   Ask students to explain why the order does matter when you subtract numbers—why, for example, $2 - 4 \neq 4 - 2$.

ADDITION: CHANGING ADDENDS, BUT NOT THE SUM

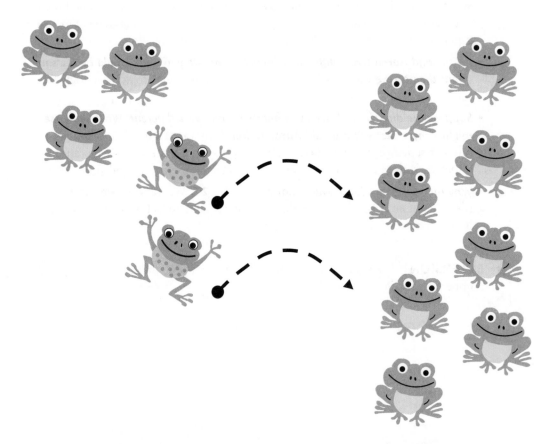

How are the number sentences you write to tell about all of the frogs the same and different after the two frogs move over?

❖ **MANY PAIRS OF NUMBERS** can be added to produce the same sum. When the pairs are analyzed, it becomes clear that if one addend is increased, the other is decreased by the same amount. This is an example of what is called the associative property for addition. For example, 9 + 2 = 7 + 4; notice that since the first addend is decreased by 2, the other is increased by 2. Essentially, the objects are divided into two piles and items from one pile are moved to the other.

Another tool that might be useful to help show this idea is the addition chart. Numbers on a bottom left to top right diagonal are all equal. As you move up one row and right one space, one addend is increased by the same amount by which the other is decreased.

+	1	2	3	4
1	2	3	4	5
2	3	4	5	6
3	4	5	6	7
4	5	6	7	8

Questioning about relating addends with the same sum should focus on why and how one sum can be changed to another to simplify a calculation. For example, knowing that $8 + 5 = 10 + 3$ makes it easier to add. The sum is the same because items are just moved around; the total never changes. Using this strategy to simplify calculations is first addressed in **Common Core State Standards 1.OA**.

The picture provided here emphasizes how the reduction of one addend by the same amount by which another is increased is really a reorganization of an amount; the total does not change.

? **QUESTIONS** to supplement the question with the picture and to include in a conversation about the picture include

* *How would the sentence change if 4 frogs had moved over?* [We want students to realize that the first addend would decrease by 4 instead of 2 and the second would increase by 4 instead of 2. The sum would not change.]

* *Why did the sum have to be the same for both sentences?* [We want students to realize that the total number of frogs had not changed, so even though the parts change, the whole (i.e., the sum) does not.]

* *Which number in the addition decreased? By how much? Which increased? By how much?* [We want students to notice that the increase in one addend matches the decrease in the other.]

* *Why do 5 + 8 and 3 + 10 have the same answer? Why might it be useful to change 5 + 8 to 3 + 10?* [We want students to know why this knowledge would be useful in allowing an addition to be done quickly either on a 100-chart or using mental math.]

◆ **EXTENSION**   Ask students to list a number of combinations that add to 14 and to tell what they notice about the various possibilities they create.

ADDING OR SUBTRACTING 10

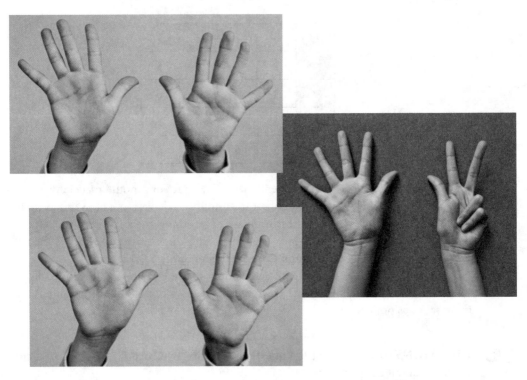

When you include or take away an extra 10 fingers, what about the total number of fingers does not change? Why?

❖ **MENTAL ADDITION OR SUBTRACTION** is simplified significantly when students realize that adding 10 simply involves increasing the tens digit by 1, or that subtracting 10 involves decreasing the tens digit by 1. Using those ideas, it becomes relatively easy, for example, to add 40 to 35 by increasing the tens digit of 35 by 4.

Questioning about adding or subtracting 10 should focus on why it is the tens digit that changes by 1 and only 1, and why adding or subtracting 10 has no effect on the ones digit of a number. It might be valuable to use 10-frames or base ten blocks to help convey this message. Adding or subtracting 10 affects the number of full 10-frames or base ten rods, but not the number of partially full 10-frames or ones blocks. Another useful tool for adding and subtracting 10 is the 100-chart. Students notice that adding 10 means going down a row and subtracting 10 means going up a row; since all the digits in a column have the same ones digit, only the tens digit is affected.

1	2	3	4	5	6	7	8	9	10
11	12	13	14	15	16	17	18	19	20
21	22	23	24	25	26	27	28	29	30
31	32	33	34	35	36	37	38	39	40
…									

The use of a mental strategy for adding or subtracting 10 is first addressed in **Common Core State Standards 1.NBT**.

Because students are so comfortable with the idea that fingers are a way to represent 10, the picture helps students see that it is tens that change, and not the 8 ones showing on the hands at the right, when all of the fingers are counted.

? **QUESTIONS** to supplement the questions with the picture and to include in a conversation about the picture include

- *Why is only the tens digit affected when you add 10?* [We want students to think about adding or subtracting as combining or separating like terms. Adding a ten or subtracting a ten affects the number of tens, but not the number of ones (or hundreds).]

- *How is the tens digit affected when you add 10?* [We want students to realize that adding 1 ten increases the tens digit by 1, while adding, for example, 3 tens increases the tens digit by 3.]

- *What digits are affected when you subtract 10, and how are they affected? Why might you have predicted this?* [We want students to realize that subtracting 10 has an effect that is very similar to adding 10 and why.]

◆ **EXTENSION**   Ask students to think about how digits change when 9 is added or subtracted instead of 10.

SUBTRACTION AS TAKING AWAY

Decide how many cookies are probably on the plate. What number sentence would you use to describe what happened when Caelan took his cookies?

TYPICALLY, STUDENTS FIRST THINK about subtraction as taking away. They need to learn that when we write the sentence $a - b = c$, we are suggesting that we began with a items, we removed b of them, and c items remain. Many students mistakenly write, for example, $3 - 5 = 2$ to mean that they took 3 items from 5 and 2 were left; although they understand the idea, it is important that they learn to write the numbers in the proper order, because at some point, they will learn that $3 - 5 = -2$.

Questioning about subtraction as take away should focus on the various processes that can be used to determine what is left and how the sentence is recorded. In particular, it is useful for students to learn that they can count back as long as they are careful not to count the original total. For example, for $9 - 2$, they would need to say the numbers 8, 7 as items 1 and 2 are removed. If a student starts by saying 9, he or she is likely to think the answer is 8 rather than 7. It is also important to have a method to keep track of how many have been taken away, so this amount must directly, or indirectly, be counted. Another method students can use is to simply take away items and then count to see how many are left. The concept of subtraction as take away is first addressed in **Common Core State Standards K.OA**.

The picture provided here shows the situation after items have been removed rather than showing the total. Students will need to recognize that the total is calculated by putting together what has been removed with what remains. This emphasizes the relationship between addition and subtraction.

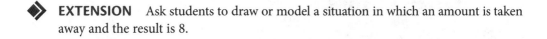

QUESTIONS to supplement the question with the picture and to include in a conversation about the picture include

- *What does the first number in your number sentence tell about? What about the other numbers in the sentence?* [We want students to recognize the role of each number in a subtraction number sentence.]

- *How would your number sentence change if the boy had taken away 4 cookies?*

- *How would your number sentence change if there were still 8 cookies on the plate?*

- *Which number is greatest in the number sentence? Why?* [We want student to recognize that the total is always greatest in this real-life type of situation.]

- *Which number is least? Does the number that is taken away always have to be least in a subtraction sentence?* [We want students to realize that if you take away a lot, you end up with a little, but if you take away a little, you might end up with more than you took away.]

- *Why might someone use a minus sign instead of a plus sign in their number sentence?* [We want students to relate the subtraction sign with a take away situation.]

EXTENSION   Ask students to draw or model a situation in which an amount is taken away and the result is 8.

SUBTRACTION TO COMPARE

What does 12 – 8 tell you about the insects?

❖ **ALTHOUGH STUDENTS TEND** to associate subtraction with take away, it is important for them to learn that we use subtraction to compare items to decide how much more one amount is than another. For example, to find out how much older one child is than another, we subtract their ages.

The subtraction model for comparing is quite different from that for take away. When modeling take away, we see the total and then remove items; we do not model both numbers in the subtraction. For example, for 8 – 2, we show 8 and then remove 2. But when we compare 8 and 2 to model how much more 8 is than 2, we normally show both the 8 and the 2 and then look at the "extra."

Questioning about subtraction as comparison should focus on the model used, what each number in the subtraction sentence represents, and why subtraction can be thought of as comparison. In this case, we would look at how many more ladybugs than butterflies there are. The concept of subtraction as comparison is first addressed in **Common Core State Standards 1.OA**.

The picture of ladybugs and butterflies is deliberately arranged as it is so that students themselves can recognize that putting the creatures into 1-1 correspondence would help them answer the question.

❓ QUESTIONS to supplement the question with the picture and to include in a conversation about the picture include

- *Where do you see 12 in the picture?* [We want students to associate the parts of the number sentence with the appropriate parts of the real-life situation.]

- *Where do you see 8?*

- *Why do you think a subtraction sentence was used?* [We want students to recognize that subtraction can tell how much more one amount is than another.]

- *When you take 8 away from 12, you see the 8 items within the 12 items. Why does it make sense to show all 8 + 12 (or 20) items to compare the ladybugs to the butterflies?* [We want students to understand why the models for take away subtraction and comparison subtraction might be different.]

- *Why is thinking about how many more ladybugs there are than butterflies like taking away 8 butterflies from the 12 ladybugs?* [We want to build a connection between the various meanings of subtraction. For example, if we think of matching the ladybugs and the butterflies, we could take away the 8 ladybugs that have a matching butterfly and see how many ladybugs do not have a match.]

◆ EXTENSION   Ask students to put out 5 blue counters and a lot more red ones, and then to tell how many more are red than blue. Ask them how they know, and have them record the associated subtraction sentence.

RELATING ADDITION AND SUBTRACTION

Does this picture show addition or subtraction or both?

❯❯ IN EARLY GRADES, students learn that we apply the operation of addition to situations where items are combined. They also learn that subtraction and addition are related. In fact, whenever there is an addition situation (e.g., 6 + 3 = 9), there is automatically a subtraction situation (e.g., 9 − 3 = 6), since a subtraction is a way of asking what must be added to one number to get another number.

Questioning about the meaning of addition and subtraction should focus on what each operation represents, how each operation relates to real-world situations, and how the two operations are related to each other. The concepts of addition and subtraction are first addressed in **Common Core State Standards 1.OA**.

The picture provided here is designed to show how different addition and subtraction sentences involving 5, 8, and 13 can be constructed and to demonstrate the notion that when you look at a static situation, you cannot tell if it represents an addition situation or a subtraction situation. The picture shows that $5 + 8 = 13$ and $8 + 5 = 13$ or that $13 - 5 = 8$ and $13 - 8 = 5$. Some students will look at this in other ways. For example, a student might suggest that it would be subtraction if some boats were removed or addition if some helicopters were added. Allow those responses, but make sure some students address the picture as it is.

❓ QUESTIONS to supplement the question with the picture and to include in a conversation about the picture include

- *What addition sentences describe the picture?* [We want students to associate combining with addition and to recognize how addition sentences describe what is being combined.]

- *What subtraction sentences describe the picture?* [We want students to associate determining one part in a whole when the other part is known with subtraction and to recognize how subtraction sentences describe the partitioning.]

- *Why can you write both kinds of sentences for the picture?* [We want students to firmly understand that every addition situation can also be viewed as a subtraction situation, and vice versa.]

- *What do all of the sentences you wrote have in common?* [We want students to note that each sentence used the same three numbers, but in a different way.]

◆ EXTENSION   Ask students to draw a picture that could be represented by both of these number sentences: $7 + 6 = 13$ and $13 - 7 = 6$.

NAMING TWO-DIGIT NUMBERS

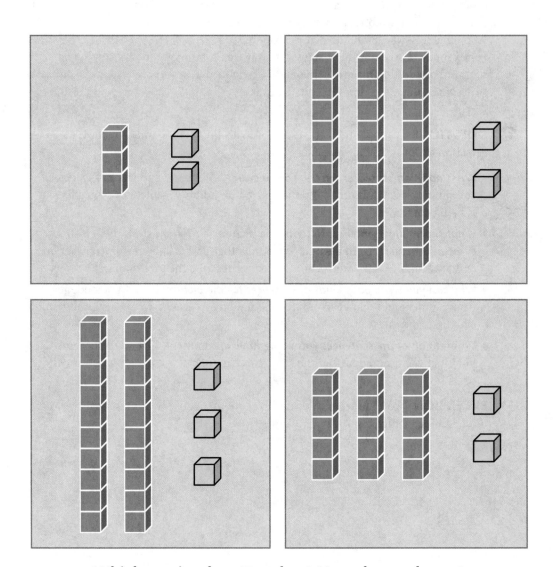

Which section has 32 cubes? How do you know?

STUDENTS MUST RECOGNIZE that it is the first digit of a two-digit number that tells how many tens there are and the second digit that tells the number of ones. Without that convention, there would be no way of distinguishing between what 32 and 23 mean. One of the fundamental ideas about counting an amount represented by a two-digit number is that we count as many groups of 10 as we can, and then we describe the leftover amounts.

Questioning about the naming of two-digit numbers should focus on what each digit tells us about the number and what it does not and should bring the student's attention to the fact that the first digit does not represent that number, but ten times that number. Thus, for example, in 32, the 3 is not 3, it is 3 tens or 3 x 10. Questions should also explore how the amounts are counted. The naming of two-digit numbers is first addressed in **Common Core State Standards 1.NBT**.

The picture provided here deals with some of the fundamental ideas about the place value system that students must understand, and it explicitly addresses some of the misconceptions students typically have about what the digits of a number represent. For example, some children view 32 as 3 + 2 = 5; some confuse the tens and ones digits; and some do not sufficiently focus on the fact that the 3 represents groups of tens, and not just groups of some random size.

? **QUESTIONS** to supplement the questions with the picture and to include in a conversation about the picture include

- *What numbers do the sections that do not have 32 cubes show?* [We want students to recognize that each picture shows a different number. We also want to observe whether students count by tens (an important place value skill) when naming 32 and 23, or by fives when describing the picture with 17 cubes.]

- *Why might someone think the other sections have 32 cubes?* [We want students to recognize that the 3 and the 2, which are represented somehow in all of the pictures, provide important information about a number.]

- *In the section with 32 cubes, why do the 3 stacks have to have 10 cubes in a stack instead of some other number?* [We want students to be aware that our place value system is built on a 10-for-1 trading rule.]

- *How would you show 41 cubes?* [We want students to generalize what they see in this picture to other numbers.]

- *How would a cube picture for 40 cubes be different from the pictures already on the page?* [We want students to confront the notion of 0 as a placeholder.]

◆ **EXTENSION**   Have students use pairs of digits to create two numbers (e.g., 4, 1 to create 41 and 14) and model those numbers with linking cubes.

NAMING THREE-DIGIT NUMBERS

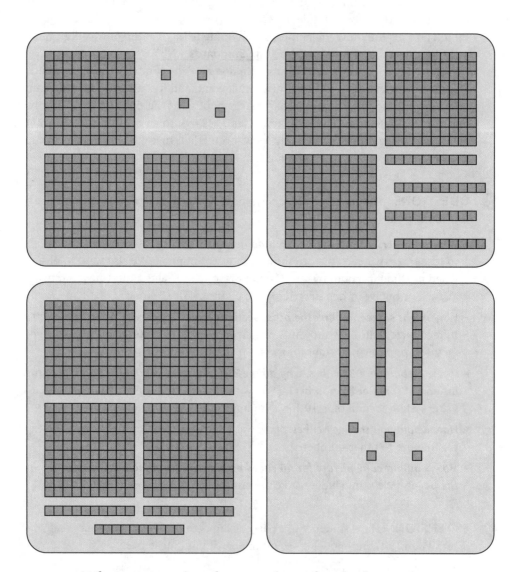

When you write the numbers for each section, how are the numbers alike and how are they different?

AS STUDENTS BEGIN to work with three-digit numbers, they learn that the left-most digit represents considerably more than the rightmost digit. This is hard for some students to recognize, particularly if they are accustomed to representing numbers using counters on a place value chart rather than using proportional materials like base ten blocks. On a place value chart, the 3 counters in the hundreds column (representing 300) do not really look any different from the 3 counters in the ones column (representing 3 ones).

Questioning about the naming of three-digit numbers should focus on what each digit tells us about the number and what it does not, and on the need for a 0 as a placeholder sometimes. The naming of three-digit numbers is first addressed in **Common Core State Standards 2.NBT**.

The picture provided here gives visual cues for students to help them see the role of each digit in the three-digit number describing each amount.

? **QUESTIONS** to supplement the question with the picture and to include in a conversation about the picture include

- *Why was the first number 304 and not 34?* [We want students to realize that without the 0, we would not have realized the 3 represented hundreds rather than tens.]

- *If you had recorded the digits 3 and 4 in the hundreds and ones columns of a place value mat, do you still think it would be important to show the 0?* [We want students to recognize that the reason we need the 0 as a placeholder is because we do not label the digits of a number with their place value.]

- *What do you think it means when we call 0 a placeholder?* [We want students to assign some meaning to the term *placeholder*, which we often use.]

- *Which two of the four numbers shown do you think are most alike? Why?* [We want to know what meanings these numbers have for the students.]

- *Why do only three of the numbers have a 0 in them?* [We want students to recognize that conventionally we do not use zeroes to the left of a whole number, so placeholders are only needed in the positions to the right of the leading digit.]

- *What does the digit on the right end of a three-digit number tell you about the number?* [We want students to recognize what each digit in a three-digit number tells us.]

- *Which digit in the three-digit number do you think is most important? Why?* [We want students to realize that the leading (leftmost) digit of a number gives us the most insight into its size.]

- *How would a picture for 403 look different from the pictures already shown?* [We want students to generalize what they have deduced from this discussion to another situation.]

◆ **EXTENSION**   Have students use base ten blocks to model a variety of three-digit numbers where only two types of blocks are used. In each case, have students draw the arrangement and record the value of the number represented.

PLACE VALUE: GROUPING IN TENS

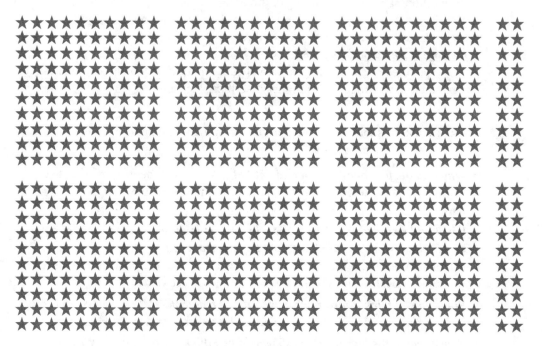

How does the arrangement of stars help make it easier to count them?

A VERY IMPORTANT IDEA for students to learn is that one of the reasons we group objects in tens, hundreds, thousands, etc., is to make it easier to count large quantities. For example, students use base ten blocks as shown below to model 146.

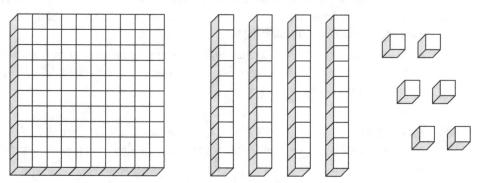

This makes it much easier to determine the total than would be the case if 146 ones were used. This concept is addressed in **Common Core State Standards 2.NBT**.

The picture provided here is designed to focus students on the fact that it is easier to count large sets if the items are grouped in 100s and 10s than if they are arranged in other ways. Ideally students will notice that there are 6 sets of 100 stars and 4 sets of 10 stars. Students should realize that they do not have to count the large groups to know there are 100 items in each, as long as they realize there are 10 rows and 10 columns. They can count 1, 2, 3, 4, 5, 6 hundreds, then 610, 620, 630, and 640 to get the full total. They might even relate what they see to base ten flats and rods.

? **QUESTIONS** to supplement the question with the picture and to include in a conversation about the picture include

- *How could you quickly tell that there are more than 600 stars?* [We want students to notice that there are 600 in just the left part of the picture.]

- *How does the arrangement of the stars make it easier for you to tell how many there are?* [We want students to articulate that the groups of 100s and 10s make it easier to count the stars.]

- *What if some groups were 100s, some 50s, and some 10s? Would it still be easy to count the stars?* [We want students to notice that other subgroups that are easy to count are also possible, although they cannot be counted as easily as if they were all 10s or 100s or even 50s.]

- *What if some groups were 100s, some 45s, some 4s, and some 2s?* [We want students to notice that some combinations do not simplify counting as much as others.]

◆ **EXTENSION**   Ask students to find a way to quickly count the number of squares on a piece of grid paper.

PLACE VALUE: POSITIONS

Why aren't these numbers the same?
They all include 1, 2, and 3.

WE USE A PLACE VALUE SYSTEM so that we can manage to use only ten digits, 0–9, to represent any whole number of any size. We just move the digits to different positions so that they represent different amounts. Using a tens digit allows us to represent numbers greater than 9; using a hundreds digit allows us to represent numbers greater than 99, etc. One of the fundamental ideas is that a digit is worth a different amount in a different position. But we do not write our numbers on place value charts; we expect students to internalize the system of reading numbers without the support of column headings.

Questioning about place value positions should focus on how the value of a digit changes depending on whether it is to the left or the right in a number, and what the values of the digits in different places actually are. The concept of place value involving hundreds is first addressed in **Common Core State Standards 2.NBT**.

The picture provided here does not actually show amounts of the various sizes, but just the numerals. Students need to have abstracted principles of the place value system to answer the question posed.

? **QUESTIONS** to supplement the question with the picture and to include in a conversation about the picture include

- *What is the 3 worth in each number?* [We want students to know the difference between the 300, 30, and 3 values for the digit 3 in the three numbers.]

- *Make up another number with a 2 where the 2 is worth the same as it is in 321. Does the number have to have three digits?* [We want students to know that the only way a 2 can have the same value as in 321 is if the 2 is the tens place. So as long as that condition is met, the 2 could be part of a two-digit, three-digit, or even larger number.]

- *Is a 1 worth more if it's to the left or to the right in a number? Why?* [We want students to recognize that digits to the left are worth more.]

- *Why do you think we call our system a place value system?* [We want to familiarize students with the term *place value* but, more importantly, we want them to recognize that the placement of a digit in a number matters as much as what the digit is.]

◆ **EXTENSION**   Ask students to draw a picture to show how the 2 in 218 is worth a different amount than the 2 in 128.

COMPARING SIZES OF NUMBERS

Which section has more marbles?
How can you be sure?

❖ **STUDENTS ARE OFTEN TAUGHT** that you determine which of two numbers is greater by counting digits or by comparing the greatest digits, then the next ones, if necessary, etc. While these rules are correct for whole numbers, not all students really understand why they work. Ideally, students recognize that one number is greater than another if it comes later in the counting sequence. This can be established if there is a number that comes between the two given numbers. For example, we know that 82 is greater than 35 because another number—such as 50—is between them; 82 comes after 50, but 35 comes before it.

Questioning about comparing whole numbers should focus on why one number is or is not greater than another, without just stating rules. Comparing three-digit numbers is first addressed in **Common Core State Standards 2.NBT**.

The picture provided here deliberately obscures the exact values. In order to help students to come to an understanding of a general principle, it is often valuable to avoid a situation that allows them to focus too much on one specific example.

? QUESTIONS to supplement the questions with the picture and to include in a conversation about the picture include

- *How do you know that one number is more than 400, but one is less?* [We want students to realize that the benchmark of 400 is useful for comparing these two particular numbers.]

- *How does knowing that help you decide which amount is greater?* [We want students to realize that if an in-between number can be found (in this case, 400 because one picture has four bags with 100 marbles each and the other has only three full 100-marble bags), the set of marbles that is greater than that in-between number is the greater number.]

- *Why does it not matter that the last bag in the first picture is more full than the last bag in the second picture?* [We want students to understand why it is only the hundreds digits, and not the tens digits or ones digits, that influence which of the two numbers is greater in this case.]

- *Why is it true that only the number of bags labeled 100 matters this time?*

- *What would other sets of bags that represent an amount between these two look like?* [We want students to generalize this idea to another situation.]

◆ EXTENSION   Have students choose pairs of numbers and, for each one, indicate what in-between number would help them decide which of their two numbers is greater.

FRACTIONS: HALVES

Why can halves look so different?

❖ **THE FIRST FRACTION** that makes sense to most students is the fraction $\frac{1}{2}$, also called *half* or *one half,* Many students, though, have a limited conception of half; they assume that an object must be divided into two identical parts for those parts to be considered halves. However, the parts need not be simple, and in fact they can be quite complex; all that matters is that their areas are equal if they are to represent half of a flat shape. For example, the rectangle below is divided in half because the white and the blue areas are equal, even though this is not obvious.

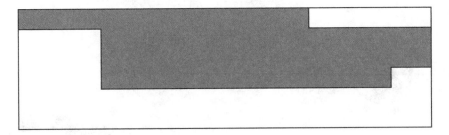

Questioning about creating halves of areas should focus on area relationships. The fraction one half is first addressed in **Common Core State Standards 2.G**.

The picture provided here uses both familiar and simple examples of one half as well as more complicated ones. The less obvious pictures are designed to provoke curiosity about what when we actually can use the term *half*.

? **QUESTIONS** to supplement the question with the picture and to include in a conversation about the picture include

- *Which picture is easiest for you to call one half? Why?* [We want students to start in a comfortable place to show their understanding.]

- *How could you check to make sure that the pictures really do show halves?* [We want students to understand that the term *half* is only applied when the parts have equal area.]

- *Can one half be made up of more than one piece of a whole?* [We want students to recognize that half means sharing fairly, but does not limit how the whole could be divided up.]

- *How do you know that there are even more possible pictures to show a half of a circle?*

◆▶ **EXTENSION**   Have students use square tiles of two colors to build a rectangle shape. Half of the rectangle should be each color.

FRACTIONS: QUARTERS

Which things in the picture would be called quarters?
Why do they have that name?

❖ **THE FRACTION** $\frac{1}{4}$, sometimes called *one quarter* and sometimes *one fourth*, is another important fraction for students to fully grasp. But many students are confused about why we use the term *quarter* for the coin as well as to represent a portion of a whole. It helps them to understand that we use the term *quarter* whenever there are four equal parts and we are talking about one of those parts. The picture provided here emphasizes this idea.

Questioning about quarters should focus on the fact that the whole is divided into four equal parts. The fraction one fourth is first addressed in **Common Core State Standards 2.G**.

? **QUESTIONS** to supplement the questions with the picture and to include in a conversation about the picture include

- *What makes the piece of chocolate one quarter, or one fourth, of the bar?* [We want students to associate the terms *quarter* and *fourth* with four equal pieces.]

- *Would the piece of chocolate on the right still be one quarter or one fourth if the piece on the left was bigger than it is now?* [We want students to recognize the importance of the pieces being equal in some way, whether area, volume, length, value, etc.]

- *What would one quarter or one fourth of four cookies be? Why?* [We want students to extend their understanding of dividing a whole to dividing a set.]

- *What is it about the dollar bill that is divided into four equal parts in the picture?* [We want students to recognize the attribute of value as being the meaningful feature in this instance.]

- *Why would it not make sense to call a nickel a quarter of a quarter?* [We want students to realize that it is because *four* coins make a dollar—and not just *some* coins making a dollar—that we use the term *quarter*. Clearly, there are five nickels and not four in a quarter.]

◆ **EXTENSION**   Have students think about what other names the penny, nickel, and dime might have been given that would make their names more like the name of the quarter coin.

MEASUREMENT: MEANING OF LENGTH

Which picture shows something long?

⯬ **AS STUDENTS LEARN** about the attribute of length, we tend to focus on straight, extended lines. However, students sometimes need to compare lengths when one line is bent or when the two lines are facing in a different directions. They need to learn that they must either straighten one line and extend it, or turn one line in order to compare it to the other. They also need to recognize that the term *long* could apply to horizontal or vertical distances.

Questioning about the concept of length should focus both on the vocabulary we use—*long, short, longer, shorter, high, taller,* etc.—and on the notion that length measures can be deceiving when the item is not already straightened out. The attribute of length is first addressed in **Common Core State Standards K.MD**.

The picture provided here is designed to emphasize that the word *long* might be used when an item is high or when an item, like the coiled snake, does not look long but actually is.

? QUESTIONS to supplement the question with the picture and to include in a conversation about the picture include

- *Would you call the ruler long?* [We want students to justify their interpretation of the word *long*. Eventually, they need to understand that the word is always relative; they might think about the ruler as compared to other rulers they might imagine or they might think of it in comparison to other objects. It is also useful to discuss whether students think that the three parts of the picture are separate (not similarly scaled), and whether or not the snake, girl, and ruler can be compared to each other based only on the picture.]

- *Would you call the girl long? What word would you use?* [We want to establish that people might use the term *tall* rather than *long*, but that it really has the same meaning—there is more length than one might expect. Some students might say she is short, but some justification should be required whether the student calls her tall or short. In fact, this is an excellent opportunity to bring out the fact that without a benchmark in the picture, you really cannot tell.]

- *Would you call the snake long?* [We want students to recognize that they need to mentally "straighten" the snake to describe its length.]

- *How could you decide if the snake is longer than the ruler?* [We want students to consider how to compare two lengths that are not already set up with matching ends.]

- *How could you decide if the girl is longer than the snake?*

◆ EXTENSION   Have students draw a picture of something that is long but does not look like it is.

MEASUREMENT: EFFECT OF UNIT SIZE

This puddle is
10 steps wide.

This puddle is
12 steps wide.

Who is right?

WE ENCOURAGE STUDENTS to use a variety of measurement units for each type of measurement attribute because we want them to recognize that we deliberately choose units so that the measurement values are meaningful. Knowing that something is 100 paper clips long does not give us as good a sense of its size as knowing that it is about 3 rulers long. We change units because we want values we can visualize.

Questioning should bring out that there is always another possible unit to use, that using a bigger unit leads to a smaller numerical value or a smaller unit to a greater value, and that comparing descriptions of the same measurement using different units can help us predict how the units are related. For example, knowing that one person measures a distance as 12 units and another as 10 units means that the first unit is a little less than the second. Although the context used in the picture focuses on length, it is desirable for students to see that the same would be true with other measurement attributes, such as area, volume, capacity, time, etc. Measuring length using different units is first addressed in **Common Core State Standards 2.MD**.

The picture provided here affords students the opportunity to see why small items might be measured in inches or centimeters and larger items in feet or meters.

QUESTIONS to supplement the question with the picture and to include in a conversation about the picture include

- *How did do you think the girl decided the puddle was 12 steps wide?* [We want students to think about the unit used when measuring and how it would be used.]

- *If she did it again, do you think she would get 12 again?* [We want students to know that when we use nonstandard units, measurements might vary somewhat, but not a lot.]

- *Could both people be right?* [We want students to know that measurements that sound different can both be correct; for example, 12 inches and 1 foot could describe the same item. Some students might think the girl measured a different width of the puddle. Acknowledge that possibility, but ask if it is possible to get that number if she had measured exactly the same part of the puddle as the boy.]

- *What if a really big man measured the puddle with his steps? What number do you think he would get? Why?* [We want students to think about how the unit relationship affects the numerical value of the measurement.]

- *What if a really small toddler measured the puddle with her steps? What number do you think she would get? Why?*

- *Are steps a good unit to use to measure length?* [We want students to know that nonstandard units might not be as meaningful to a person as standard units.]

EXTENSION   Ask students to describe as much as they can about a situation in which someone says that a pitcher of water would fill 20 cups and someone else says it would fill 12 cups.

MEASUREMENT: STANDARD UNITS OF LENGTH

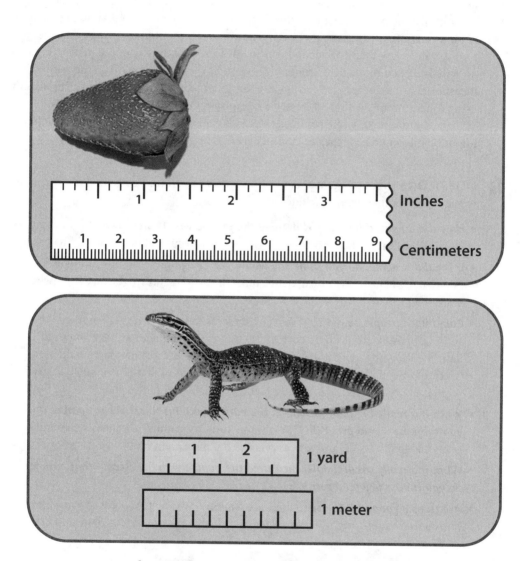

Why might you use different tools to measure different objects?

⩔ **STUDENTS LEARN** to use standard units of measurement to make communication easier. They learn several possible units because some are more appropriate in certain situations than others.

We want students to understand that the individual who is measuring has freedom to choose a unit, but that using a shorter unit for small lengths and a longer unit for longer lengths ensures that the numerical values of the measurement are meaning-ful. For example, telling someone that an object is 100 inches long is less meaningful than saying it is about 8 feet long.

Questioning about standard units should focus both on the names of the length units we typically use, both metric and Imperial, and on the tools we use to support measurement in each of those types of units. The concept of standard length units is first addressed in **Common Core State Standards 2.MD**.

The picture provided here (the parts of which are not drawn to scale) is designed to emphasize that centimeter and inch rulers make sense to use when measuring small things, and meter and yard sticks are better suited for measuring larger things.

? **QUESTIONS** to supplement the question with the picture and to include in a con-versation about the picture include

- *Why are rulers good things to use to measure length?* [We want students to understand that a tool for measuring length should highlight the attribute of length.]

- *How is the ruler for measuring the strawberry different from the rulers for measuring the lizard?* [We want students to observe that the units associated with the long and short rulers are different.]

- *Could you measure the strawberry with the long ruler? Why might you not do that?* [We want students to recognize that you can measure a short thing with a long tool, but that it would be hard to describe the length in terms of the larger units.]

- *Could you measure the lizard with the short ruler? Why might you not do that?* [We want students to recognize that you can measure a long thing with a short tool, but it would be inconvenient because it would have to be used over and over so many times.]

- *How are inches like centimeters? How are they different?* [We want students to recognize that there are several standard units that are appropriate for measuring small lengths.]

- *How are inches like yards? How are they different?* [We want students to recognize the difference between short and long units,]

◆ **EXTENSION**   Have students decide what other objects they might measure with each of the pictured tools.

2-D SHAPES VERSUS 3-D SHAPES

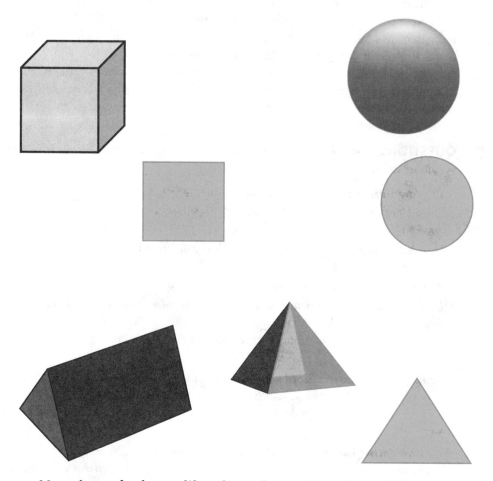

How is each shape like the others? How is it different?

MANY STUDENTS CONFUSE 2-D shapes with similar 3-D shapes. We want students to realize that 2-D shapes and 3-D shapes are fundamentally different even though they might have certain features in common. 3-D shapes are not flat, but they share features with 2-D shapes, such as corners (vertices), edges, and surfaces (although there is only one surface for 2-D shapes). Students look at both 2-D and 3-D shapes in early grades, as specified in **Common Core State Standards K.G**.

The picture provided affords an opportunity to directly confront errors students typically make when identifying 3-D shapes. They often call spheres circles, cubes squares, and triangular prisms or pyramids triangles, most likely because they are more familiar with the names for the 2-D shapes.

? **QUESTIONS** to supplement the questions with the picture and to include in a conversation about the picture include

- *What features do the square and cube both have?* [We want students to attend to the similarities between shapes, for example, the types of corners, the types of side lengths, the regularity, etc.]
- *What features do the pyramid, triangle, and triangular prism all have in common?*
- *What features do the circle and sphere both have?* [We not only hope that students recognize that both shapes are curved or round, but maybe that both have a center point equally far from all the points on the edges.]
- *How are the square, circle, and triangle alike?* [We want students to recognize the 2-D shapes as flat or single-faced.]
- *What is another shape, not in the picture, that you think is more like the square, circle, and triangle than the other shapes?*
- *How are the cube, the sphere, and the triangular prism alike?* [We want students to recognize the 3-D shapes as having depth.]
- *What is another shape, not in the picture, that you think is more like the cube, sphere, triangular prism, and pyramid than the other shapes?*
- *Why does it make sense that there are different names for each shape in the picture?* [We want students to recognize the value, for communication, of different shapes having different names.]

◆ **EXTENSION** Have students use modeling clay to build some 2-D and some 3-D shapes. They can discuss various attributes of the shapes they build.

COMPARING 2-D SHAPES

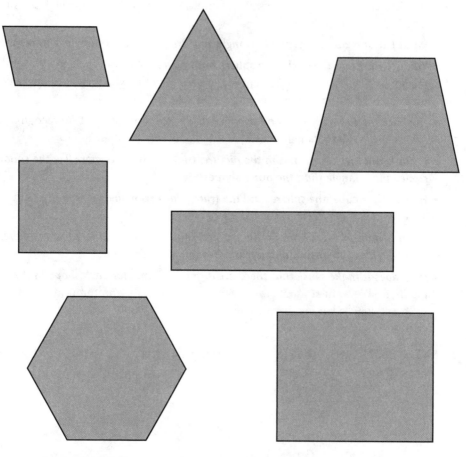

Which frames do you think are most alike?

❖ **STUDENTS BEGIN TO LEARN** that properties of shapes can and are used to distinguish one shape from another, usually leading to a different name for each type. Some of the shapes students learn about in early grades are triangles, squares, rectangles, hexagons, and trapezoids, although other shapes (such as the parallelogram) are also informally introduced. Students look at some of these shapes as early as in kindergarten, according to **Common Core State Standards K.G**.

The picture provided here allows students to compare a broad variety of shapes so that many attributes can be considered, including numbers of sides, whether or not the sides look like they are the same length, whether the shapes are narrow or not, what the corners look like, the sizes of the shapes, etc.

❓ QUESTIONS to supplement the question with the picture and to include in a conversation about the picture include

- *Which shapes do you think are most alike? Why those?* [We want students to articulate properties of shapes they consider when comparing them.]

- *Which shape do you think is most like the hexagon? Why?* [We want students to realize that the number of sides is only one of the many attributes that one might consider when comparing shapes.]

- *Which four-sided shape do you think is the most unlike the others? Why?* [We want students to realize that measurement attributes such as area, side length ratios, or angle types might be considered.]

- *How is the triangle like the square?*

- *Do you think the size of the shape should influence the name of the shape?* [We want students to recognize that the overall size of a shape, unlike the relative side lengths or ratio of side lengths, does not affect the name of the shape.]

◆ EXTENSION   Have students draw two shapes with different names that they think are a lot alike and tell why they think that.

COMPARING 3-D SHAPES

Which two objects do you think are most alike? Why?

⩔ **ONE OF THE THINGS** students learn when working with 3-D shapes is that there are both measurement (e.g., height, width, depth) as well as geometric (e.g., face shapes, nature of the vertices, etc.) aspects to consider and compare. Students look at simple 3-D shapes as early as in kindergarten, according to **Common Core State Standards K.G**.

The picture provided here models several common 3-D shapes. The heights were made equal so that students would focus more on the geometry than on the measurement aspects of the shapes in deciding which shapes are most alike.

? **QUESTIONS** to supplement the questions with the picture and to include in a conversation about the picture include

- *Why might someone pick the drum and the ball?* [We want students to consider various properties of these shapes, for example, whether they roll or not.]

- *Why might someone pick the warning sign and the tent?* [We want students to consider various properties of these shapes, for example, whether or not there are triangular faces.]

- *Which two shapes do you think are the most different? Why?* [We want students to choose properties to contrast—numbers of faces, edges, etc.; whether the shapes roll or not; how symmetric the shapes are; etc.]

- *Which of the shapes in the picture do you think a cereal box is most like? Why?* [We want students to think about other shapes beyond those already shown.]

- *If you picked a shape of your own to be a lot like each of the given ones, but not exactly the same shape, what would you pick? Why?* [We want students to use their own imaginations and experience to relate various 3-D shapes.]

◆ **EXTENSION**   Have students use modeling clay to build two shapes they think are different in most ways but alike in one way. Ask them to articulate both the similarities and differences.

COMPOSING SHAPES

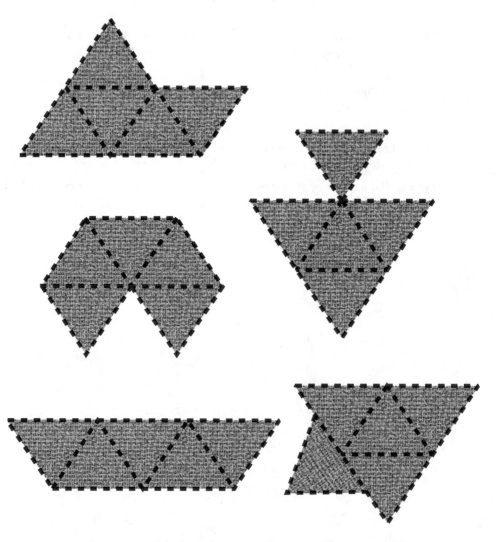

How would the shapes change if you used 6 triangles instead of 5?

❥ **COMPOSING SHAPES** involves putting together shapes to create other shapes. It is very important for students to have experience, even in the early grades, of building shapes using simpler shapes. Not only does composing shapes help students better analyze shapes they encounter but it will also get them ready for later work in measurement.

Students generally have experience putting together squares to make larger squares or rectangles, but composing other shapes is also important. Students look at how shapes can be put together initially in **Common Core State Standards K.G**.

The picture provided here has students consider how equilateral triangles can be put together in various arrangements to create different shapes. Students might consider the number of sides of the newly created shapes, how the triangles are attached to each other, how similar the final shapes are to the original triangles, or how the side lengths or the angles of the final shapes compare.

❓ QUESTIONS to supplement the question with the picture and to include in a conversation about the picture include

- *How do you know the shapes made with six triangles will have more area?* [We want students to recognize what the area of a shape represents.]

- *When you attach a new triangle, do you always add a side to the shape?* [We want students to realize that whether a side is added or not depends on the placement of the added triangle relative to the earlier shape. The new sides might actually extend or replace existing sides.]

- *You are attaching one new triangle to an existing shape. Is the result always the same no matter where you attach it?* [We want students to think about the symmetry of the original shape to see what effect the new triangle might have in different locations.]

- *Is it possible to start with two different shapes from the picture, add a triangle to each, and end up with the same shape?* [We want students to practice visualizing skills and realize that it would be possible to start with different shapes and end with the same one, depending on how the attachment is done and what the starting shapes were.]

- *Do you think there would be more possible shapes made of six triangles than five triangles? Explain.* [We want students to make geometric conjectures, explain their reasoning, and investigate their hypotheses.]

◆ EXTENSION Have students begin with four rectangles (or triangles) to see what shapes they can create. Then give them an additional rectangle (or triangle) to see how the new shapes compare to the original ones.

SHAPE PUZZLES

Why can you get different shapes when you put together the same pieces?

ONE OF THE MOST ENJOYABLE ways students can experience the composition of shapes is to create and/or solve puzzles. When they solve jigsaw puzzles, they likely do not think about how they are putting together shapes to make other shapes; they are more focused on the simple fitting together of pieces. However, when they use pattern blocks or tangrams, as shown below, to make objects, they are more likely aware that they are composing shapes to make other shapes.

Pattern block puzzles

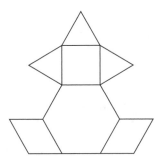

Tangram puzzles

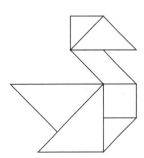

Students look at how shapes can be put together initially in **Common Core State Standards K.G**.

Questions about putting together shapes should focus on how things fit and why they fit that way, as well as the effect of alternate placements of the same shape.

The main visual provided here has students consider how the same objects, in this case a set of tangram pieces, shown at the bottom of the picture, can be put together in different ways to create different shapes. Ideally, students might be provided those pieces and asked to try to create at least one of the pictures they see.

? QUESTIONS to supplement the question with the picture and to include in a conversation about the picture include

- *What does each picture look like?* [We want students to look at the composed shapes as a whole.]

- *What shapes do you see making up each picture?* [We want students to recognize that the same set of small shapes was used each time, and what those small shapes are.]

- *In each picture, find the two large triangles that are touching. How are those arrangements different?* [We want students to explore how two shapes can be put together in different ways.]

- *There are seven pieces making up each picture. Do you think it would be harder to get different shapes if there were only five pieces?* [We want students to realize that even smaller numbers of shapes can be combined in different ways.]

- *Do you think it would be harder to have different designs if all of the small shapes we used were identical?* [We want students to consider how the symmetry of shapes might affect how different they could look when combined with other shapes.]

◆ EXTENSION   Have students use a set of four or five pattern block shapes to try to make as many different designs as they can. Have them draw each shape they make.

CHAPTER 3

Grades 3–5

MULTIPLICATION: EQUAL GROUPS

Can you write ☐ × ☐ to describe this picture?

STUDENTS ARE INTRODUCED to multiplication in this grade band as a way of describing the total count of equal groups. This understanding is critical not only to ensure that students have an understanding of what the operation of multiplication represents but also to promote the use of strategies to decompose and recompose numbers to be able to calculate with them more effectively. These skills are referenced in **Common Core State Standards 3.OA**.

In the picture provided here, most—but not all—groups are equal. However, the groups of 2 can be rearranged to form groups of 4, or the groups of 4 can be broken down into groups of 2. A lively discussion could occur if some students are adamant that the penguin picture does not show multiplication while others recognize the possibility of rearrangement. Notice how much more interesting the question is with groups of 4 and an *even* number of groups of 2 (which can be rearranged into groups of 4) than it would be if there were either all groups of 4 (where there is only one reasonable response) or many groups of 4 and an odd number of groups of 2 (where only groups of 2 would be possible and not groups of either 2 or 4). Questions that are somewhat ambiguous tend to lead to good mathematical conversations.

? QUESTIONS to supplement the question with the picture and to include in a conversation about the picture include

- *When do you use multiplication?* [We want students to realize that multiplication describes situations involving equal groups.]

- *Are all the groups of penguins the same size? Does that matter when you are deciding if you can use multiplication?* [We want students to notice sizes of groups when deciding whether or not to use multiplication.]

- *Could the penguins be rearranged into equal groups?* [We want students to see that sometimes rearranging groups can change the way we describe them. For example, 7 + 9 can be rearranged to 8 + 8, which is a double, which might help us calculate the sum, but the fact that there was a double was not immediately obvious.]

- *Is it easier to rearrange the penguins as shown here into equal groups than it would have been if there had been five icebergs with two penguins on them?* [We want students to see that we could still have created equal groups of 2, but no longer equal groups of 4.]

◆ EXTENSION   Ask students to create a different picture, using different numbers of items, that does not look like a multiplication situation at first glance but really is.

MULTIPLICATION: COMMUTATIVITY

Which pictures make it easy to see that 3 × 4 = 4 × 3?
Which do not?

❖ **KNOWING THE COMMUTATIVE PRINCIPLE** for multiplication will cut the number of multiplication facts students need to learn almost in half. It will also help them to be more flexible in numerical calculations. Organizing sets in an array makes it easier for students to see a number of principles, including the commutative and distributive principles.

The picture provided here is designed to show that

- $a \times b = b \times a$, but it is not always easy to see why
- if a set of equal groups is shown in an array formation, it is easier to see why $a \times b = b \times a$

The value of commutativity is referenced in **Common Core State Standards 3.OA**.

This picture is designed to contrast three situations: one where an array is used so that commutativity of multiplication is very clear (since 4 rows of 3 is clearly 3 columns of 4); one where it is not too difficult to pull out 3 groups of 4 (the conductors, flute players, and cellists), even though the visual really only shows 4 groups of 3; and one where it is more challenging to find the 3 groups of 4 among the 4 groups of 3. Ideally students should be able to distinguish the three situations by the end of the classroom discussion.

? **QUESTIONS** to supplement the questions with the picture and to include in a conversation about the picture include

- *What does the 4 tell you about each of the three pictures? What does the 3 tell you about each picture?* [We want students to realize that a factor could be the number of groups or the size of a group.]

- *How are the pictures alike?* [We want students to see that there are many ways to represent 4 groups of 3, including the array.]

- *How are the pictures different?* [We want students to see that some visual representations of mathematical ideas make it easier to see principles than do other visual representations. For example, in the diagrams below, the one on the left makes it easy to see why you can add the same amount (the one dark square) to both numbers (4 and 8) without changing the difference, but the picture on the right does not makes it as easy.]

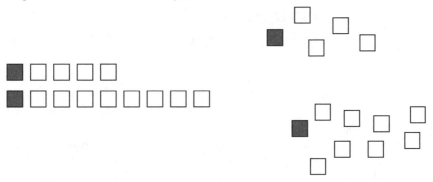

♦ **EXTENSION**   Ask students to create a picture that makes it easy to see why $3 \times 2 = 2 \times 3$. Then ask them to create a picture where it is less obvious.

MULTIPLICATION: THE DISTRIBUTIVE PRINCIPLE

How does the picture help you see that there are lots of ways to figure out what 7 × 6 is?

❖ **BEING FAMILIAR** with the distributive principle for multiplication will, in the short term, help students to learn new facts by using known facts. Actually, knowing the facts for 5 and the facts for 2, along with the distributive principle, would allow a student to efficiently figure out any unknown fact. For example, 7 × 8 could be 5 × 8 + 2 × 8, or 6 × 9 could be 5 × 9 + 9. In the longer run, the distributive principle will be of immense importance to students as they learn to multiply one digit by multi-digit numbers—for example, 6 × 53 = 6 × 50 + 6 × 3—and still later in algebra—for example, 2(x + 4) = 2x + 8.

Distributivity can be extended to include subtraction as well. For example, to determine 9 × 7, a student could calculate 10 × 7 and subtract 1 × 7. This is particularly useful when one of the factors is slightly less than a multiple of 10.

The picture provided here is designed to show that a strategy for multiplying two numbers is to break one of them into parts, multiply each of the parts by the other factor and add the results. For example, 7 × 6 can be calculated as 7 × 4 + 7 × 2 (each group of 6 is 4 + 2, so 7 groups of 6 is actually 7 groups of 4 and 7 groups of 2), as 7 × 5 + 7 × 1, as 7 × 3 + 7 × 3, or as 5 × 6 + 2 × 6 (7 groups is the same as 5 groups and 2 more groups), 4 × 6 + 3 × 6, or 6 × 6 + 1 × 6. This property is referenced in **Common Core State Standards 3.OA**.

The carrots in the picture provided here are arranged in an array to make it easier to see that either factor can be broken up into subpieces. If a different arrangement had been used, it might have been fairly easy to see, for example, that 7 × 6 = 2 × 6 + 5 × 6.

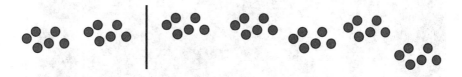

Some students might realize that a factor can be divided into more than two parts. For example, 7 × 6 is 7 × 2 + 7 × 2 + 7 × 2 since 6 = 2 + 2 + 2.

? **QUESTIONS** to supplement the question with the picture and to include in a conversation about the picture include:

- *What multiplications does the picture show?* [We want students to notice both the 7 rows of 6 but also the 7 rows of 4 + 7 rows of 2.]

- *How can you rearrange the rows or columns to show other ways to figure out 7 × 6?* [We want students to know that any combinations of rows or columns could be used.]

- *What does the picture tell you about how you can figure out multiplication facts you don't already know?* [We want students to realize that knowing smaller facts can help them with bigger facts.]

◆ **EXTENSION**   Ask students to create a picture that makes it easy to see why 8 × 7 is 5 × 7 + 3 × 7.

MULTIPLICATION: 2-DIGIT BY 2-DIGIT

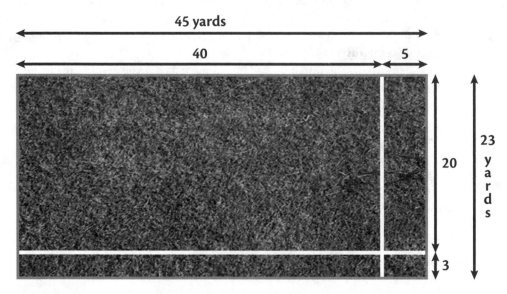

45 yards

40   5

20   23 yards

3

How do the white lines help you figure out the grass area?

❦ **THIS PICTURE IS DESIGNED** to show that an area model based on place value can be useful to help a student multiply two 2-digit numbers. This is referenced in **Common Core State Standards 4.NBT**. This builds on the distributive principle for multiplication in a very particular way.

By multiplying 23 × 45 as (20 + 3) × (40 + 5), the four sub-products of 20 × 40, 20 × 5, 3 × 40 and 3 × 5 can all be calculated mentally before they are added; this makes the calculation simpler. As well, the student actually sees why we multiply 23 by 45 the way that we do.

The diagram below suggests an algorithm (procedure) that could become the student's primary approach to multiplying two 2-digit numbers. Each number could be broken up into tens and ones. For example, for 37 × 74, the student might draw:

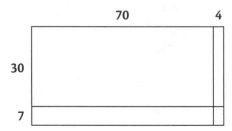

70   4

30

7

He or she would calculate the area of each section (2100, 120, 490, and 28) and add those values.

86

Later, the very same approach can be used to model two algebraic expressions, for example, the area $(3x + 2)(x + 1)$ as the product of the length and width, $3x + 2$ and $x + 1$.

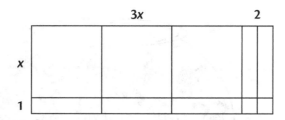

? **QUESTIONS** to supplement the question with the picture and to include in a conversation about the picture include

- *Why does determining the area of the grassy field in the picture represent a multiplication?* [We want students to know that multiplications can be represented by areas of rectangles because a rectangle's area can be broken up into rows (or columns) of equal size.]

- *What are the areas of each of the four sections?* [We want students to recognize the various subproducts of a product.]

- *Why is it easier to multiply 20 × 40 in your head than 23 × 45?* [We want students to see the value of breaking up the original factors into particular subproducts.]

- *Why was it a good idea to break up 23 as 20 + 3 instead of as 17 + 6?*

- *How would you use the same idea to multiply 39 × 42?* [We want to see if students can generalize what they learned.]

◆ **EXTENSION**   Ask students to create a picture that might help them multiply the 3-digit number 120 by the two-digit number 42.

DIVISION AS EQUAL GROUPS OR SHARING

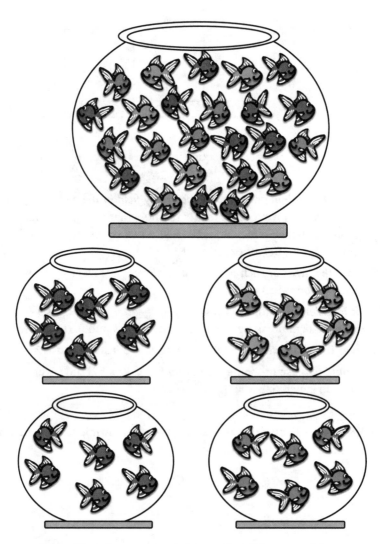

What division story does the picture show?
Suppose there were 4 more fish.
Would it still show a division story? How?

◈ **STUDENTS NEED TO LEARN** that division is used in two different situations, both involving the creation of equal groups. In one instance, the number of groups is known and the division is used to determine the size of each group (sometimes called "partitive" or "sharing" division). For example, if you know there are 24 fish and you want to split them equally into 4 bowls, you want to determine the number of fish to put in each bowl. But in the other instance, the size of the group is known and the objective is to determine the number of equal groups that can be formed (sometimes called "quotative" or "measurement" division). For example, if you know there are 24 fish and you want to create groups of 6 fish, you would determine the number of fish bowls needed by dividing. This concept is referenced in **Common Core State Standards 3.OA**.

The picture provided here allows for both of these meanings of division to emerge. Some students will think of 24 ÷ 4 and others will think of 24 ÷ 6 when looking at the picture. Coloring the fish using four different colors was deliberate to help students more easily see not only 4 groups of 6, but also 6 groups of 4.

The second question, asking about 4 additional fish, is designed to help students see that by adding 4 fish there is still a division story. Either, there are 4 bowls and now there are 7 fish in a bowl, or there are groups of 7 and now there are 4 of those groups.

? QUESTIONS to supplement the questions with the picture and to include in a conversation about the picture include

- *How does the picture show 24 ÷ 6?* [We want students to look at the quotative meaning of division.]

- *How does the picture show 24 ÷ 4?* [We want students to look at the partitive meaning of division.]

- *What multiplication does the picture also show?* [We want students to recognize the relationship between multiplication and division.]

- *Why is every division picture also a multiplication picture?*

- *What would the division have been if 8 fish had been added?* [We want students to realize the effect on the quotient of adding to the dividend.]

◆ EXTENSION   Ask students to create a multiplication picture. Then ask whether there is also a division picture in their picture and, if so, what it is.

DIVISION: REMAINDERS

Where are the remainders in each picture?
What does "remainder" mean?

❖ **THE CONCEPT OF REMAINDER** is a critical one when learning about division. Students must realize that when forming groups of a given size or equal groups, it may not be possible to use all of the items and still have equal groups; there is sometimes a remainder. This concept is referenced in **Common Core State Standards 4.OA**. Later students learn that remainders can be handled in different ways, sometimes as fractions or decimals (e.g., $18 \div 4$ as $4\frac{1}{2}$ or as 4.5). When students first start dividing, however, the remainder is often left as a whole amount called a remainder (e.g., $18 \div 4$ as 4 R 2).

The picture provided here is designed to emphasize that the remainder can be the same no matter the total size of the sample or the size or number of equal groups. In this instance, the remainder is 1 whether dividing 10 by 3 or 13 by 4 (or 3) or 16 by 5 (or 3).

? **QUESTIONS** to supplement the questions with the picture and to include in a conversation about the picture include

- *How are the pictures alike and different?* [We want students to notice the common remainder.]

- *What division sentences would you write to describe each picture?* [We want students to identify the dividend and divisor and recognize that a remainder must be included with the quotient.]

- *How would the pictures be different if the remainders had been 2? How would the division sentences be different?* [We want students to realize that the divisor need not change, but the dividend would.]

- *Why couldn't all of the remainders have been 3?* [We want students to understand why the remainder must be less than the divisor; otherwise, the group size or number of groups could have been larger.]

- *What is the greatest remainder possible when you divide by 5? Why?*

- *What would it mean if the remainder were 0?* [We want students to recognize that a remainder of 0 suggests a "perfect" division.]

- *Can you have the same remainder when you divide by different amounts?* [We want students to understand that the remainder is not determined by just the divisor or just the dividend, but a combination of the two.]

◆ **EXTENSION**   Ask students to draw very different-looking pictures where a division is shown each time and the remainder is always 4.

ROUNDING NUMBERS

GUESS the Number of CANDIES in this JAR!!!
Answer: 426 Candies

GUESS HOW MANY CANDIES!!!

Which would you say:

- **About 400 candies?**
- **About 430 candies?**
- **About 425 candies?**

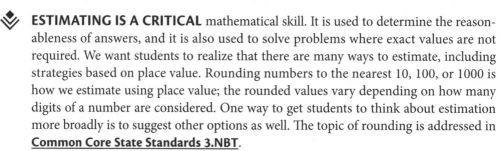

ESTIMATING IS A CRITICAL mathematical skill. It is used to determine the reasonableness of answers, and it is also used to solve problems where exact values are not required. We want students to realize that there are many ways to estimate, including strategies based on place value. Rounding numbers to the nearest 10, 100, or 1000 is how we estimate using place value; the rounded values vary depending on how many digits of a number are considered. One way to get students to think about estimation more broadly is to suggest other options as well. The topic of rounding is addressed in **Common Core State Standards 3.NBT**.

The picture provided here is designed to enable students to consider whether rounding to the nearest 100, to the nearest 10, or to the nearest 25 makes the most sense in a given situation.

? QUESTIONS to supplement the questions with the picture and to include in a conversation about the picture include

- *Why might you say 400 but not 500?* [We want students to know that when you round to the nearest 100, you choose whichever multiple of 100 is actually nearer.]

- *Why might you say 430 rather than 420?* [We want students to know that when you round to the nearest 10, you choose whichever multiple of 10 is actually nearer even if the tens digit changes.]

- *Why might you say 425? Why not?* [We want students to realize that you don't have to estimate using a multiple of 10.]

- *When might you say 400 instead of 430?* [We want students to know that when you do not want to or need to be as precise, you can estimate using fewer digit values.]

- *Would you ever say 450?* [We want students to know that we could estimate to the nearest 5 or 50 or 500.]

◆ EXTENSION   Ask students to choose several numbers that could be estimated in different ways. Then have them describe the different ways to estimate and when they think each would make the most sense.

PLACE VALUE:
MULTIPLYING AND DIVIDING BY POWERS OF 10

**Suppose there were eight butterflies to
look at through the kaleidoscope.
How many butterflies would you see in the viewer?**

❖ **MULTIPLYING BY 10, 100, OR 1000** is a required skill for multiplying multi-digit numbers. It is extremely helpful for students to realize that these calculations can be handled using mental math and that the calculations are based on place value.

For example, to multiply 3 × 52, a student needs to multiply 3 × 50; this is accomplished by multiplying 3 × 5 by 10. This topic is tied in with **Common Core State Standards 4.NBT**.

The picture provided here is designed to motivate discussion that will lead students to see that multiplying by 10 has the effect of moving the number of original items from the ones place in a place value chart to the tens place. For example, 8 × 10 changes 8 ones to 8 tens.

Thousands	Hundreds	Tens	Ones
			8
		8	0

This is because what used to be just 1 item turns into 10 items. The 0 in the ones place is included as a way to show that the 8 is now in the tens column, not the ones column.

? **QUESTIONS** to supplement the question with the picture and to include in a conversation about the picture include

- *How many butterflies would you see in the viewer if the viewer showed 100 butterfly images for each real butterfly?* [We want students to see the parallel between multiplying by 10 and multiplying by 100.]

- *How many butterflies would you see in the viewer if the viewer showed 1000 butterfly images for each real butterfly?* [We want students to see the parallel between multiplying by 10, by 100, and by 1000.]

- *Is it easy to predict how many images you would see in the viewer if you know the original number of butterflies? How would you do that?* [We want students to articulate the "rule" for multiplying by 10, by 100, or by 1000.]

- *Would you ever see exactly 37 objects in the viewer? Explain.* [We want students to apply the rule for multiplying by 10 in reverse to see why the result has to end in 0 when using whole numbers.]

◆ **EXTENSION**   Ask students to consider the effect of dividing by 10, by 100, or by 1000.

PLACE VALUE: RENAMING NUMBERS

DAILY SPORTS

3400 Fans Attend First Game of the Season!!

**If the people sat in stands of 100 people,
how many stands would have been full?
How many rows of 10 people would have been full?**

WE FREQUENTLY REPRESENT numbers in more than one way. For example, we might think of 1900 as 19 hundreds or as 1 thousand and 9 hundreds. We might think of 150 as 15 tens (e.g., 15 dimes) or 1 hundred and 5 tens (e.g., 1 dollar and 5 dimes). This is important for several reasons.

One reason is that it might help in computational situations. For example, realizing that 150 is 15 tens might make it easier to divide it by 10 (15 tens ÷ 1 ten = 15). It also helps students see why 5 × 3.4 has the same digits as 5 × 34; it is because 5 × 3.4 is actually 5 × 34 tenths. Another reason for thinking of numbers in more than one way is that it might help in number comparisons. For example, recognizing that 230 is 23 tens might make it easier to explain why it is more than 220, or 22 tens. This topic is addressed in **Common Core State Standards 4.NBT**.

The picture provided here is designed to enable students to see that 3400 is not only 3 thousands and 4 hundreds, but also 34 hundreds or 340 tens. It reminds students that we build numbers by making groups of tens, hundreds, or thousands. It also helps them notice that if a number is modeled as a group of hundreds, it could also be modeled as 10 times as many tens.

? QUESTIONS to supplement the questions with the picture and to include in a conversation about the picture include

- *How does it help to think of 3400 as 34 hundreds?* [We want students to understand that there are 34 groups of 100 in 34 hundreds.]

- *How does it help to think of 3400 as 340 tens?* [We want students to realize that there are 340 groups of 10 in 340 tens.]

- *Why were there more tens than hundreds?* [We want students to realize that if the group sizes are smaller, more groups are required. In fact, if a group is one tenth of the size of another group, then 10 times as many of the smaller groups are needed.]

- *How else could you describe 400 tens? How do you know?* [We want students to apply the idea already explored to other situations.]

- *Is it easier to name numbers that end in zeroes in more ways than numbers that don't? Explain your thinking.* [We want students to see that it is easier to rename numbers ending in zeroes as tens, hundreds, thousands, etc. However, students may think that 401 is easy to rename, too, as 40 tens and 1 one or as 4 hundreds and 1 one.]

◆ EXTENSION   Ask students how to rename $30,000 to make it easier to answer each question: How many thousand dollar bills would it take to make up that amount? Hundred dollar bills? Ten dollar bills?

FACTORS: WHAT THEY ARE

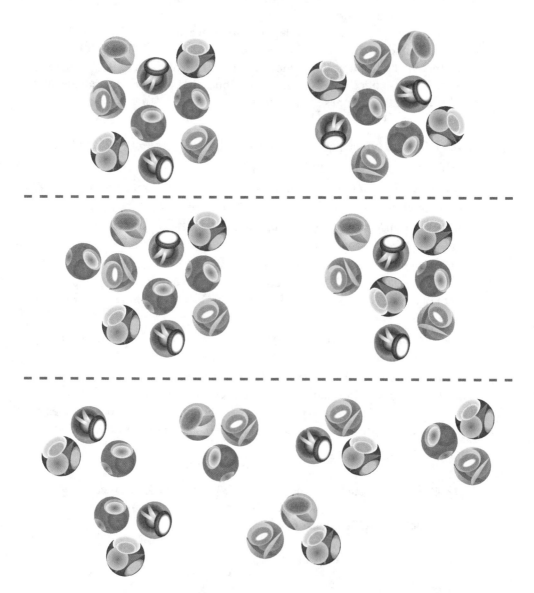

How many people could share 18 marbles fairly?

⬇ **FAIR SHARING** of whole numbers involves finding factors of numbers. For example, 1, 2, 3, 4, 6, 8, 12, or 24 people can fairly share 24 items, since each of those numbers is a factor of 24. Only 1, 2, 13, or 26 people could fairly share 26 items. Finding factors relates closely to work with multiplication and division.

It is important that students learn that the least factor of a whole number is always 1 and the greatest factor is always the number being factored. The topic of finding factors is addressed in **Common Core State Standards 4.OA**.

The picture provided here is designed to encourage students to see that there are generally several or even many ways to share a given amount. They will notice that some ways of sharing (i.e., fair sharing) lead to factors and other ways of sharing do not.

? QUESTIONS to supplement the question with the picture and to include in a conversation about the picture include

- *What is the greatest number of people who could share the marbles?* [We want students to recognize that the greatest factor of a number is the number itself.]

- *What is the fewest number of people who could have the marbles?* [We want students to recognize that the least factor of a number is 1.]

- *If there were more marbles, which of those numbers would change? Why?* [We want students to understand that the least factor never changes (it is always 1), although the greatest factor changes with the number.]

- *What number of people could not share the 18 marbles fairly?* [We want students to realize that some numbers do not qualify as factors.]

- *For any given amount, is there always a number of people who could not share it fairly?* [We want students to realize that unless a whole number is 2, there are always numbers less than that whole number that are not factors.]

◆ EXTENSION   Ask students to imagine there was a different number of marbles that could be shared in the same number of ways as 18 marbles. Ask what that number could be. (Some answers are 12, 50, 98, 28, ...)

FACTORS COME IN PAIRS

How do you know that 6 dogs could also share 24 bones fairly?

AS STUDENTS TRY TO FACTOR numbers, it helps them to realize that factors come in pairs. For example, if 8 is a factor of a number (e.g., 8 is a factor of 48), then the number divided by 8 is also a factor (i.e., 48 ÷ 8 = 6). Sometimes we show this using a factor "rainbow" as shown on the next page for 48. This reduces the amount of work necessary to calculate all factors.

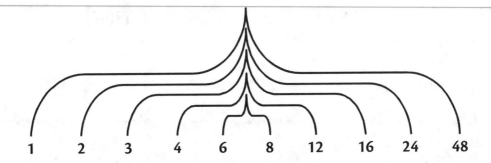

Factoring is addressed in **<u>Common Core State Standards 4.OA</u>**.

The main picture provided here is designed to enable students to see that if 24 is shared among 4, another factor is the share size, which is 6. This is because division has both a "sharing" and a "how many groups" meaning. The specific question is geared to helping students see that we can go back and forth between these two kinds of meaning.

? QUESTIONS to supplement the question with the dog bone picture and to include in a conversation about it include

- *What other numbers of dogs could share 24 bones fairly?* [We want students to realize that 24 could have other factors and to look for them.]

- *How did the picture help you figure this out?* [We want students to realize, for example, that if you have 4 groups, you could combine groups to get another factor (2), or, in this case, since the size of the group is even, you could split each group into two parts, resulting in 8 groups, or 8 as a factor. Each time, there is an automatic second factor.]

- *Why does getting one factor of a number automatically give you another one?* [We want students to realize that you can always divide the whole by the size of the equal groups to get another factor, the number of equal groups.]

- *Would the factors still come in pairs if there had been 25 bones?* [We want students to realize that sometimes the partner of a factor is the factor itself (e.g., 5 × 5), so there are not distinct pairs, but there still are pairs.]

◆ EXTENSION   Ask students to make factor rainbows for different numbers and decide which numbers have an even number of factors and which have an odd number of factors.

FRACTIONS: REPRESENTING

What does this picture show about fractions?

❖ **THE TOPIC OF FRACTIONS** is a complex one for students because fractions have so many meanings and the meanings are all about a relationship between two numbers (the numerator and denominator) as opposed to being about a single quantity. This topic is addressed in **Common Core State Standards 3.NF**.

The picture provided here is designed to show students that the fraction $\frac{3}{4}$ could mean $\frac{3}{4}$ of a single area (or whole) or $\frac{3}{4}$ of the items in a group. It also emphasizes that when we talk about a fraction as applied to a group, the items in the group need not be identical. This is a cause of confusion for many students, who might be comfortable saying that $\frac{3}{4}$ of the circles in the top row of the diagram on the next page are dark, but not that $\frac{3}{4}$ of the shapes in the bottom row of the diagram are circles (because the square is bigger), even though it is true.

? **QUESTIONS** to supplement the question with the picture and to include in a conversation about the picture include

- *How are different parts of the picture similar?* [We want students to realize that many different types of objects or groups can be split into four equal parts.]

- *How are they different?* [We want students to realize that sometimes fourths describe parts of sets, sometimes parts of areas, sometimes parts of capacities, etc.]

- *How would the fractions describing the different parts of the picture all be the same?* [We want students to realize that no matter what the whole is, when it is divided into four equal parts and three of those parts are under consideration, then we use the fraction $\frac{3}{4}$.]

- *Are all $\frac{3}{4}$s the same size?* [We want students to realize that $\frac{3}{4}$ describes a relationship between parts and a whole and gives no indication of the size of the parts or the whole.]

- *When you see $\frac{3}{4}$, why do you also see $\frac{1}{4}$?* [We want students to recognize that the only way to know that an amount is $\frac{3}{4}$ is to either see the whole or have the whole implied. If the whole is present or implied, the missing part, the $\frac{1}{4}$, is also either present or implied.]

- *How many more ways could you think of to represent $\frac{3}{4}$?* [We want to encourage students to think of other wholes that could be divided into fourths. Possibilities are alternate areas (wholes) or sets, but also masses, volumes, time units, or other measures.]

◆ **EXTENSION**   Ask students to draw different sorts of pictures to show what $\frac{2}{5}$ means. Then ask which of their pictures they think makes it easiest to see $\frac{2}{5}$ and why.

FRACTIONS: EQUIVALENCE

How can you describe the cabinet using fractions?

◈ **A CRITICAL SKILL** in students' development of fractional understanding is the recognition that fractions have many names, often referred to as "equivalent fractions," and that sometimes one of the alternate names might be more useful in a particular situation than another. For example, if one were asked for a fraction just a little bit more than $\frac{2}{3}$, it might be helpful to know that $\frac{2}{3} = \frac{20}{30}$ and use the fraction $\frac{21}{30}$. Also, once students learn to add and subtract fractions, or even divide them, it is useful to have equivalent names for those fractions so that common units can be used.

Students will eventually realize that a way to get an equivalent fraction is to subdivide each existing section into equal subsections. For example, the picture below shows why $\frac{1}{2} = \frac{2}{4}$ or $\frac{3}{6}$.

To get equivalent names for $\frac{1}{2}$ using a "part of a set" model, a picture like the one below, where a circle mat is shown beneath the counters, is more convincing than just using the counters.

The topic of equivalence is addressed in **Common Core State Standards 3.NF**.

The picture of the set of drawers is designed to show students that eighths might be renamed as fourths (by looking at "columns") or as halves (by looking at "rows").

? **QUESTIONS** to supplement the question with the picture and to include in a conversation about the picture include

- *Which fractions that you said are worth the same amount?* [We want students to know that we compare parts to a whole no matter what the parts and whole are.]

- *How could you design a cupboard to show that $\frac{3}{4} = \frac{18}{24}$?* [We want students to recognize that if each fourth had 6 drawers instead of 2, $\frac{3}{4}$ would have to look like $\frac{18}{24}$. In other words, students realize that the parts of the whole can all be divided into equal sections to give an equivalent fraction.]

- *How many more fractions do you think are equal to $\frac{3}{4}$? Why?* [We want students to understand that there is an infinite number of equivalent names for a fraction because the parts can be divided into any number of equal subsections.]

◆ **EXTENSION**   Ask students to draw a picture that would help someone see lots of names for $\frac{2}{3}$.

FRACTIONS: COMPARING

Monday	Tuesday	Wednesday	Thursday
☀	🌧	☀	☀

Monday	Tuesday	Wednesday	Thursday	Friday
☀	☀	☀	☀	🌧

Monday	Tuesday	Wednesday	Thursday	Friday	Saturday
☀	☀	🌧	☀	☀	☀

Monday	Tuesday	Wednesday	Thursday	Friday	Saturday
☀	☀	🌧	🌧	☀	☀

What fractions would you compare to decide which group of days seems the sunniest?

⬇ **COMPARISON OF FRACTIONS** is an important skill. For example, students may need to know whether $\frac{2}{3}$ of a set is more or less than $\frac{3}{4}$ of that same set. Although fraction comparison is easy for students when the denominators are the same, they need to use other strategies if the denominators are different. For example, they learn that if two fractions have the same numerator, e.g., $\frac{3}{7}$ and $\frac{3}{8}$, the one with the greater denominator is actually less (since there are the same number of pieces, but the pieces are smaller); they also learn that fractions can be compared by using benchmarks such as $\frac{1}{2}$ or 1 (e.g., $\frac{3}{7} < \frac{4}{5}$, since $\frac{3}{7}$ is less than $\frac{1}{2}$ and $\frac{4}{5}$ is more than $\frac{1}{2}$) or by using equivalent fractions with the same denominator. The topic of fraction comparison is addressed in **Common Core State Standards 3.NF**.

Students can use the first three rows of days to see that fractions such as $\frac{3}{4}, \frac{4}{5}, \frac{5}{6}$, etc.—where the numerator is one less than the denominator—get closer to 1 as the values of the numerator and denominator increase. They can use rows 2 and 4 to see that $\frac{4}{6} < \frac{4}{5}$, since 6 is greater than 5. And they can use rows 3 and 4 to see that $\frac{4}{6} < \frac{5}{6}$, since 4 is less than 5.

? QUESTIONS to supplement the question with the picture and to include in a conversation about the picture include

- *What fraction of sunny days might be less than all of the ones shown? Did you change the numerator or denominator of the original fractions, or both?* [We want students to realize that decreasing a numerator or increasing a denominator makes a fraction smaller, or that if a fraction has a very small numerator and a large denominator, it has to be very small.]

- *What fraction of sunny days might be greater than all of these? Did you change the numerator or denominator of the original fractions, or both?* [We want students to realize that increasing a numerator or decreasing a denominator makes a fraction larger, or that if a fraction has a large numerator that is only one less than its denominator, it has to be very close to 1.]

- *What groups of days would you use or draw to show that $\frac{5}{6} < \frac{7}{8}$?* [We want students to recognize the roles of both the numerators and the denominators when comparing fractions.]

◆ EXTENSION Ask students to discuss how they would decide the order of size for this set of fractions: $\frac{3}{5} \frac{2}{5} \frac{3}{4} \frac{8}{9} \frac{1}{8} \frac{3}{7}$.

FRACTIONS: MIXED NUMBER/
IMPROPER FRACTION RELATIONSHIP

How many whole apples, pears, and lemons were cut up?
How do you know?

BECAUSE STUDENTS HAVE ASSOCIATED the concept of fractions with parts of something, it becomes difficult for many students to deal with improper fractions, which are more than a whole. A further complication is that teachers often forget to explicitly identify the whole, so (for example) a student might not know whether to call the shaded portion in the diagram on the next page $1\frac{1}{2}$ or $\frac{3}{4}$; it all depends on whether the whole is one rectangle or both.

Yet one more issue is that we normally use mixed numbers, and not improper fractions, in conversation. We might say that something measures $1\frac{1}{2}$ yards, but would rarely, if ever, say $\frac{3}{2}$ yard. The introduction of improper fractions and their mixed number equivalents is implicit in **Common Core State Standards 4.NF**.

The picture provided here uses everyday objects so that the whole is more obvious in each case. Shown are $2\frac{1}{2}$, $3\frac{1}{2}$, or $4\frac{1}{2}$ wholes. Because of the way the fruits are modeled, thinking of the amounts as $\frac{5}{2}$, $\frac{7}{2}$, or $\frac{9}{2}$ also makes sense.

? **QUESTIONS** to supplement the questions with the picture and to include in a conversation about the picture include

- *How does the picture show that 5 halves = $2\frac{1}{2}$? That 7 halves = $3\frac{1}{2}$? That 9 halves = $4\frac{1}{2}$?* [We want students to relate improper fractions to mixed numbers.]

- *How do you know that for each type of fruit there are a whole number of fruits and another half?* [We want students to associate an even number of halves with a whole number and an odd number of halves with a whole number plus an additional half.]

- *What else does the picture show?* [We want students to learn to look at a situation and extract as much information as possible. For example, a student could say that if there were another half, there would be a whole number. Or a student could say that each time there are two more halves, there is one more whole.]

- *Suppose each of the items pictured was cut in half. What fractions would be showing then?* [We want students to recognize that cutting halves in halves yields fourths, so we might call the fractions fourths, but there would still be the same amount of fruit.]

◆ **EXTENSION**   Ask students to draw pictures to make it easy to see the mixed number names for $\frac{5}{3}$, $\frac{8}{3}$, and $\frac{11}{3}$.

FRACTIONS: COMMON DENOMINATORS

**You are going to combine the juice from different glasses,
and you have to predict how full the glasses will be afterward.
Which amounts are easiest to predict? Why?**

❖ **AS STUDENTS BEGIN** to perform operations with fractions, it becomes increasingly important that they can look at two fractions and see why and how it is easier to combine them when they have a common denominator. Even if we do not know what ninths look like, we know that 2 ninths and 3 ninths make 5 ninths. But we have to do a lot more analysis to figure out what 2 ninths and 3 eighths might be. It is not that one cannot figure out the sum, but without the visuals or renaming fractions, it is very difficult. Considering common denominators is addressed in **Common Core State Standards 4.NF**.

The picture provided here is designed to help students notice that it is easier to combine halves with halves, thirds with thirds, etc., although it allows the possibility for students to see that a renamed $\frac{2}{4}$ is also easy to add to $\frac{1}{2}$.

No attempt is made at this point to show students how to get a common denominator. They just need to see the advantages of having one.

? QUESTIONS to supplement the questions with the picture and to include in a conversation about the picture include

- *What would you combine to show that $\frac{1}{2} + \frac{1}{2} = 1$?* [We want students to notice how easy it is to see the answer to $\frac{1}{2} + \frac{1}{2}$.]
- *What would you combine to show that $\frac{1}{4} + \frac{3}{4} = 1$?* [We want students to notice how easy it is to see the answer to $\frac{1}{4} + \frac{3}{4}$.]
- *What would you combine to show what $\frac{2}{4} + \frac{3}{4}$ is?* [We want students to see the ease of adding fractions with the same denominator even if the answer is greater than 1.]
- *Why is it hard to predict how full a glass would be if you tried to combine the $\frac{1}{2}$ and $\frac{1}{3}$ glasses?* [We want students to realize that it is hard to predict the sum of fractions with different denominators without appropriate concrete materials.]

◆ EXTENSION   Ask students to list pairs of fractions that are easy to add and then explain why they are easy to add.

ADDING FRACTIONS

Is the fraction of the children that are boys the same as the fraction of a single new pizza that could be made using only the slices with mushrooms?

AS STUDENTS LEARN to add fractions, it is important for them to recognize that they are adding parts of the *same* whole. While $\frac{1}{2}$ of an area and $\frac{1}{4}$ of that same area is $\frac{3}{4}$ of the area, it is not true that $\frac{1}{2}$ of the area of one item and $\frac{1}{4}$ of the area of another is $\frac{3}{4}$ of either area; the whole must be the same for the sum of two fractions to be meaningful. This is in contrast to the situation when ratios are combined. For example, if $\frac{2}{3}$ of one set of shapes are circles and $\frac{1}{3}$ of another set is a circle, then circles make up $\frac{3}{6}$ of the combined set, but do not make up $\frac{3}{3}$ of either set. Addition of fractions with unlike denominators is first addressed in **Common Core State Standards 5.NF**.

The picture provided here is designed to focus students on the difference between adding parts of the same whole and parts of different wholes. Although the pizzas are cut differently, they are the same size, so it makes sense to talk about combining slices to make a single new pizza the same size as the original two. The same is not true with the boys and girls; it would not make sense to talk of all of the boys being a fraction of the first or second group.

❓ QUESTIONS to supplement the question with the picture and to include in a conversation about the picture include

- *What fractions describe each of the two groups of children?* [We want students to recognize the potential addends in each situation.]

- *What fractions describe the parts of each pizza with mushrooms?*

- *When you describe the total fraction of boys, what is the whole and what are the parts?* [We want to focus student attention on consideration of the whole when fractional amounts are combined.]

- *When you describe the fraction of a single new pizza made up of only the slices already covered with mushrooms, what is the whole and what are the parts?*

- *Do you think both situations are addition situations or not?* [We want students to consider what addition situations actually refer to when fractions are combined.]

◆ EXTENSION   Ask students to draw a picture to show what they think $\frac{2}{5} + \frac{1}{3}$ means.

MULTIPLYING FRACTIONS

**A snowfather is skating with his snowchildren.
What fraction of the group is not wearing a skirt?
What fraction of the children is not wearing a skirt?**

IT IS IMPORTANT that students recognize that multiplication of fractions involves taking a part of a part and that, in fact, the part becomes the whole in the intermediate stage. For example, $\frac{2}{3} \times \frac{3}{5}$ means that $\frac{3}{5}$ temporarily becomes the whole of which the part $\frac{2}{3}$ is taken. Multiplication of fractions is addressed in **Common Core State Standards 5.NF**.

The picture provided here allows the students to see the difference between taking a fraction of a whole and a fraction of a part. Initially, they notice that 3 out of 4 of the snowpeople are not wearing a skirt, but only 2 out of 3 of the snowchildren are not, so different fractions are involved in the two related situations. We will want them to eventually associate the situation with describing $\frac{2}{3}$ of $\frac{3}{4}$ as $\frac{2}{4}$.

The picture of the snowpeople represents the idea of multiplication of fractions that are parts of sets. A similar example is based on showing a group of 2 red and 2 blue circles and 3 red and 5 blue triangles. Students could be asked what fraction of the blue shapes are triangles ($\frac{5}{7}$) or what fraction of all the shapes are blue triangles ($\frac{5}{12}$). Notice that $\frac{5}{12} = \frac{5}{7} \times \frac{7}{12}$ (which is $\frac{5}{7}$ of the fraction of all the shapes that are blue).

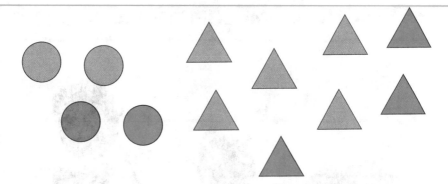

It is also possible to demonstrate the same ideas by using fractions of a whole. Students could be asked what fraction of the hexagon is striped ($\frac{1}{6}$) or what fraction of the whole shape is striped ($\frac{1}{8}$). Notice that $\frac{1}{8} = \frac{1}{6} \times \frac{6}{8}$ (which is $\frac{1}{6}$ of the part of the design that is a hexagon).

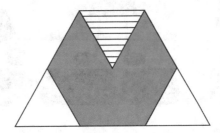

❓ QUESTIONS to supplement the questions with the picture and to include in a conversation about the picture include

- *What is the denominator of the fraction that tells the part of the group that is not wearing a skirt? Why?* [We want students to consider what the parts of a fraction tell us about a situation.]

- *What is the denominator of the fraction that tells the part of the group of snowchildren that is not wearing a skirt?*

- *Why are the denominators different?* [We want students to recognize that even within the same picture, different denominators might be used if different wholes are being considered.]

- *Why might you think of the fraction that tells the fraction of the snowchildren not wearing a skirt as $\frac{2}{3} \times \frac{3}{4}$?* [We want students to ultimately relate the product of two fractions to the notion of "of"; that is, $\frac{2}{3} \times \frac{3}{4}$ means $\frac{2}{3}$ of $\frac{3}{4}$, so, in effect, the whole has changed to the part, $\frac{3}{4}$.]

- *What would calculating $\frac{1}{3} \times \frac{3}{4}$ tell you about the picture? Why?* [We want students to apply what they just learned.]

◆ EXTENSION Ask students to draw a picture to show what $\frac{4}{5} \times \frac{5}{6}$ might mean.

FRACTIONS: MULTIPLYING AS RESIZING

One height is $\frac{7}{8}$ of another. One height is $1\frac{1}{3}$ times another. Which is which?

❖ **IT IS IMPORTANT** that students recognize that multiplying by a value, whether a whole number or a fraction, is a way to describe the effect of using a scale factor of that value. For example, multiplying by 2 means doubling a distance, just as multiplying by $\frac{3}{5}$ is the same as making each distance $\frac{3}{5}$ as long. The notion of multiplication as resizing is addressed in **Common Core State Standards 5.NF**.

The picture provided here allows students to see the effects of multiplying by a fraction less than one and of multiplying by a fraction greater than one. It focuses students on the fact that multiplying by a fraction only reduces size if the fraction is less than one.

❓ **QUESTIONS** to supplement the question with the picture and to include in a conversation about the picture include

- *What clues did you use to decide which height was $\frac{7}{8}$ of which other height?* [We want students to recognize that $\frac{7}{8}$ of something is most of it, but not all of it.]
- *What clues did you use to decide which height was $1\frac{1}{3}$ of which other height?* [We want students to recognize that $1\frac{1}{3}$ of something is all of it and another $\frac{1}{3}$.]

- *Which height is less than $\frac{7}{8}$ of which other height? How do you know?* [We want students to realize that $\frac{7}{8}$ of 1 is less than $\frac{7}{8}$ of $1\frac{1}{3}$, since the whole is bigger in the second instance. Some students might realize that the height of the shortest child is about $\frac{2}{3}$ (actually $\frac{7}{8} \times \frac{3}{4}$) times the height of the tallest child.]

- *Which height is more than $1\frac{1}{3}$ of which other? How do you know?* [We want students to realize that $1\frac{1}{3}$ of 1 is more than $1\frac{1}{3}$ of $\frac{7}{8}$, since the whole is smaller in the second instance. Some students might realize that the height of the tallest child is about $1\frac{1}{2}$ (actually $\frac{8}{7} \times 1\frac{1}{3}$) times the height of the shortest child.]

- *Why can you think of comparing heights as multiplying?* [We want students to begin to think of multiplicative comparisons to ready them for proportional thinking. In other words, even though one person may be so many inches taller than another, we want students to think about the multiplicative relationship between them, for example, that one value is twice as much or $1\frac{1}{2}$ times as much as another.]

EXTENSION   Ask students to draw three pieces of licorice where the length of one is about $\frac{2}{3}$ the length of another and where the length of one is about $\frac{5}{2}$ the length of another. Ask how else each length compares to the others and how the students know this.

FRACTIONS AS DIVISION

How much of an apple is each share?

 AT SOME POINT, we want students to realize that the fraction $\frac{a}{b}$ can be interpreted as $a \div b$. This is used both when improper fractions are renamed as mixed numbers—for example, $\frac{6}{4} = 1\frac{2}{4}$, since $6 \div 4 = 1\frac{2}{4}$—and when we have students divide a numerator by a denominator to determine a decimal equivalent for a fraction—for example, $\frac{2}{5} = 0.4$ is determined by dividing 2 by 5. Thinking of fractions as division is addressed in **Common Core State Standards 5.NF**.

The picture provided here is designed to help students see that one way to model $a \div b$ is to divide each of the a objects into b pieces, giving each of the b sharers a piece from each object. In this case, since 4 people are sharing, each of the 3 objects is divided into fourths. If each person gets one fourth from each of the three objects, the total share is $\frac{3}{4}$. Since division describes sharing, this shows why $3 \div 4 = \frac{3}{4}$.

Another way to think about why $\frac{3}{4} = 3 \div 4$ is to think of $3 \div 4$ as asking how much of a 4 fits into a 3. This is what is called the "measurement" meaning of division, analogous, for example, to how many 3s make 9 for 9 ÷ 3. Cuisenaire rods make a good model. Clearly, the 3 is $\frac{3}{4}$ of the 4.

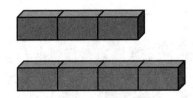

❓ QUESTIONS to supplement the question with the picture and to include in a conversation about the picture include

- *What operation would you use to write a number sentence to describe sharing the apples?* [We want students to recall what division means.]
- *How does the picture help you see that you can think of $\frac{3}{4}$ as 3 ÷ 4?* [We want students to realize that by using the denominator to decide how to split each object and the numerator to describe the number of objects, they can see both the sharing implied by the division and the fractional amount each person receives.]
- *What might a picture look like that would show that $\frac{5}{8}$ = 5 ÷ 8?* [We want students to generalize what they see in this picture to a similar situation.]

◆ EXTENSION Ask students to draw a picture to show why you can calculate 5 ÷ 6 by dividing 5 by 6.

DECIMALS: RELATING HUNDREDTHS TO TENTHS

Why does this arrangement of flowers make it easy to describe 0.2 and 0.02 of the flowers?
What other decimals of the flowers are easy to describe?

STUDENTS NEED TO BE able to compare not only decimal tenths to decimal tenths but also decimal tenths to decimal hundredths. To prepare for that, it is important that they recognize how tenths and hundredths can be related. By using an array that is 10 × 10, it is easy to see tenths as full rows (or columns) and hundredths as individual items within the array. Recognizing the difference between decimal tenths and hundredths is first addressed in **Common Core State Standards 4.NF**.

The picture provided here allows students to see the difference between 0.2 (2 tenths), the light pink flowers, and 0.02 (2 hundredths), the yellow flowers. It also provides the opportunity to see that 0.2 is also 0.20 (20 hundredths) and what 0.78 (the dark purple flowers) looks like. Some students will also suggest they see the decimal 1.0 or 1.00 if they consider the entire picture.

? **QUESTIONS** to supplement the questions with the picture and to include in a conversation about the picture include

- *Why are there two ways to use decimals to describe the light pink flowers?* [We want students to realize that 2 rows out of 10 is the same as 20 flowers out of 100, that is, just like the fraction $\frac{2}{10} = \frac{20}{100}$, the decimal 0.2 = 0.20.]

- *Are there two ways to use decimals to describe the two yellow flowers?* [We want students to realize that it is not possible to write 0.02 as tenths; some students might realize, however, that 0.02 can be written as 0.020, although it may be unlikely to come up given this particular context.]

- *Suppose a decimal was of the form 0.☐ (such as 0.4 or 0.6). What part of the picture would it describe?* [We want students to realize that tenths would describe full rows or full columns in this picture.]

- *Suppose a decimal was of the form 0.☐☐ (such as 0.23 or 0.88). What part of the picture would it describe?* [We want students to realize that hundredths represent individual flowers in this picture.]

- *What decimals can describe parts of the picture? Which can't?* [We want students to realize that decimal tenths or hundredths could describe the picture. Students are also likely to realize that decimals greater than 1 are unlikely to be used to describe the picture. It is possible, however, if for example, the students suggested that 2.0 could describe twice as much as half the flowers.]

◆ **EXTENSION**   Ask students to draw a picture where it would be easier to show tenths than hundredths. Then ask them to draw a picture where it is easier to show hundredths than tenths.

DECIMALS: EQUIVALENCE

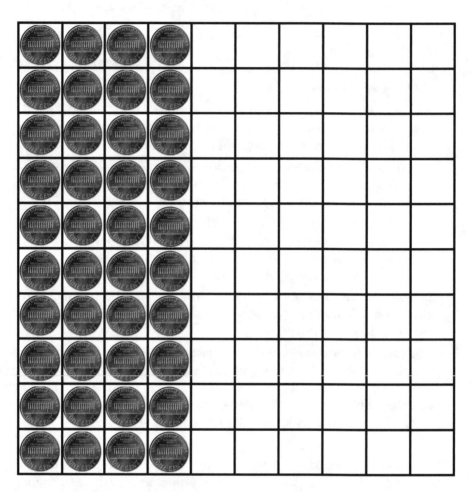

What two decimals could you use to describe how full of pennies the grid is?

⧫⧫ **JUST AS STUDENTS LEARN** to rename fractions with equivalent names to help them in situations where they are comparing or operating with fractions, the same is true for decimals. By using an array that is 10×10, it is easy to see tenths as full rows (or columns) and hundredths as individual items within the array.

It is also important that students recognize that if only tenths and hundredths are considered, then only decimals of the form ☐.☐0 (e.g., 0.20, 1.30, etc.) will have two equivalent decimal representations. Some students who might be familiar with decimal thousandths may raise the point that any decimal can be represented in more than one way by using more decimal digits (e.g., 0.42 as 0.420); but many will not think of it, and that is to be expected in Grades 3 or 4. The notion of equivalence of different decimal representations is first addressed in **Common Core State Standards 4.NF**.

The picture provided here provides students the opportunity to see that 0.4 is also 0.40 (or 40 hundredths). By connecting with money, the 0.40 makes lots of sense, while the column arrangement allows students to clearly see the 0.4.

? QUESTIONS to supplement the question with the picture and to include in a conversation about the picture include

- *What decimal describes each small square in the grid?* [We want students to recognize that when the whole has 100 parts, each part is 0.01.]

- *What coin describes a whole column? Why?* [We want students to realize that 10 pennies is worth 1 dime, so a dime describes a column.]

- *What decimal describes a whole column? Why does the answer make sense in terms of the coins?* [We want students to realize that it makes sense that a dime is represented as 0.1 of a dollar.]

- *Would you have to fill whole columns to be able to represent coins as either decimal tenths or decimal hundredths of a dollar?* [We want students to realize that tenths are groups of 10 squares, so that as long as a multiple of 10 squares are filled, whether they are full columns or not, we can write the amount as either tenths or hundredths.]

◆ EXTENSION   Ask students to choose two other equivalent decimals and to draw a picture that does not use coins to show why those decimals are equivalent.

DECIMALS: ADDING AND SUBTRACTING

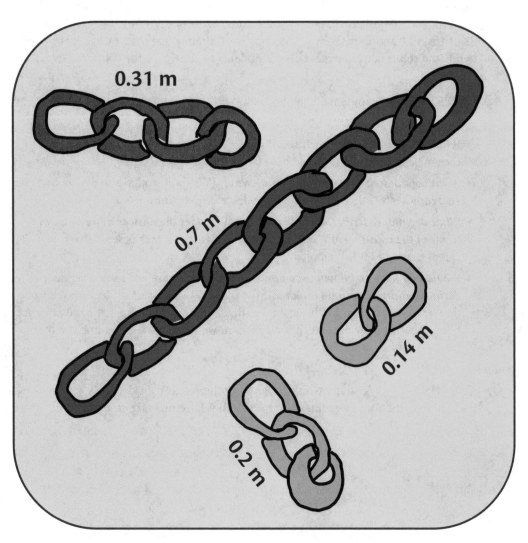

0.31 m

0.7 m

0.14 m

0.2 m

Which chains could you put together to have a total length of about 0.5 m? Why those?

AS WITH ANY OTHER type of number, we want students to recognize that adding decimals involves putting together and subtracting can involve comparisons. Students will see that even if decimals with different numbers of digits are used, there is a way to add them and to subtract them, just like whole numbers with different numbers of digits can be added or subtracted.

Questioning should bring out that it is not necessary to ensure that decimals have the same number of digits after the decimal place to add them or subtract them. For example, although 0.3 and 0.25 can be added by renaming 0.3 as 0.30, it is equally correct to think "there are 3 tenths and 2 more tenths as well as 5 hundredths; that's 5 tenths and 5 hundredths or 0.55." Similarly to subtract 0.3 – 0.25, you can think of 0.25 as halfway between 0.2 and 0.3 and that means you need another 5 hundredths, or 0.05 to get from one number to the next. Adding and subtracting decimals with different numbers of digits is first addressed in **Common Core State Standards 5.NBT**.

The picture provided here affords students the opportunity to see that combining either 0.2 and 0.31 or 0.14 and 0.31 gives a total of about 0.5, or 5 tenths. In one case, it involves 2 tenths and 3 tenths and a bit more; in the other, it involves 1 tenth and 3 tenths and a bit more.

? **QUESTIONS** to supplement the questions with the picture and to include in a conversation about the picture include

- *How did you know that you couldn't use the longest chain?* [We want students to realize that the sum of two addends is greater than either one, and 0.7 is greater than 0.5.]

- *How did you know that you couldn't use the two shortest chains?* [We want students to realize that 2 tenths and less than 2 tenths can't make 5 tenths.]

- *Could you have considered just the digits in the tenths place to answer the question?* [We want students to recognize that, when estimating, the tenths digits only can often be used. Some students will realize, though, that if the hundredths digit is too great (e.g., for 0.19), it might make more sense to consider the hundredths digit too.]

- *Why can't you just add 2, 14, 7, and 31 and put a decimal point in the front to get the total length?* [We want students to realize that if you are adding different units (i.e., some are tenths and some are hundredths), you cannot combine them without considering the unit. This is just like recognizing that 2 tens and 3 ones is neither 5 tens nor 5 ones.]

- *If you were deciding how much longer one chain was than another, which two would be easy to compare? Why those?* [Students might decide that it is easier to compare lengths when units are the same (e.g., tenths with tenths or hundredths with hundredths), but they might also have other interesting ideas on this question.]

◆ **EXTENSION**   Ask students to choose two decimals that are easy to subtract or to add and to tell why they are easy to calculate with.

MEASUREMENT: TIME INTERVALS

Was this a long nap or a short nap?

❖ **AS STUDENTS LEARN** to read clocks and tell how much time has passed, it is equally important to alert them to thinking about the relative length of that time interval—is it a long time or a short time? We want students to realize that the determination of whether an amount of time is long or short is a relative issue; the same amount of time could be viewed as a long time for certain activities but a short time for other activities.

Questioning about time duration should address strategies for deciding how long something takes, as well as comparisons to known events to decide whether that time is a long time or not and the factors that might make it a long time or not. Calculation of time duration is first addressed in **Common Core State Standards 3.MD**.

The picture provided here uses fairly simple times and a familiar situation to make it easier for students to calculate the duration and to compare it to known durations to decide whether the time is long or not.

? **QUESTIONS** to supplement the question with the picture and to include in a conversation about the picture include

- *How long did the nap last? How do you know?* [We want students to calculate the duration of the nap and also to realize that one could add or subtract to figure it out.]

- *Suppose the nap started $\frac{1}{2}$ hour later but ended at the same time. How long would it have lasted?* [We want students to relate duration to both start and end times.]

- *What might influence how long a person naps? How long do you think a typical man might nap during the day in the summertime?* [We want students to begin to relate the time described in a picture to a known personal benchmark.]

- *When else might he have started and ended his nap to have napped the same amount of time?* [We want students to realize that many start/end combinations lead to the same elapsed time.]

◆◆ **EXTENSION**   Have students choose other start and end times for various activities, calculate their durations, and decide whether the times are unusually long or not.

MEASUREMENT: AREA OF RECTANGLES

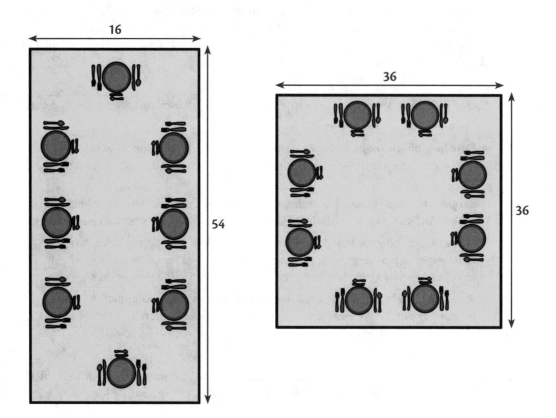

Which table has more space?

❖ **AS STUDENTS GO UP** the grades, they encounter more and more measurement formulas. One of the earliest two formulas are the formulas for the area and perimeter of a rectangle. It is important that students learn that the reason we use measurement formulas is to allow us to use simple linear measures (measures that can be taken easily using a ruler) to determine more complex measures, for which tools are less accessible or more complex to use.

Although adults are more likely to associate the term "space" with area, a student could legitimately think about the perimeter as determining how many people could sit at the table, a different kind of measure of space. Questioning should bring out that area and perimeter are different ways of describing space, that different-looking shapes can have the same perimeter, that two rectangles with the same perimeters can have different areas, and that one can use linear measures of a rectangle to determine its area. The formula for the area of a rectangle is first addressed in **Common Core State Standards 3.MD**.

The picture provided here is designed so that students will see that perimeter is a different and independent measure of a shape than its area; that is, knowing one does not tell you about the other.

? QUESTIONS to supplement the question with the picture and to include in a conversation about the picture include

- *What different things about the table could you measure?* [We want students to understand that any object has many attributes that can be measured; in this case, length, width, perimeter, and area are just some of those attributes. Others might include height off the ground (length of the legs), thickness, etc.]

- *Which measurement tells you how many items, both place settings and serving dishes, could fit on the table?* [We want students to associate the area of the rectangle with how much can fit on it.]

- *Which measurements tell you how many chairs can fit around the table?* [We want students to associate the perimeter of a rectangle with the edges of the table rather than the "inside" of it.]

- *Suppose you placed square tiles 18 units by 18 units on each table. How many would fit along each length? Each width? How many would cover the whole table? Why?* [We want students to start relating the area of the rectangle to its linear dimensions using simpler values.]

- *If you wanted to measure the areas of the table tops in squares 1 unit on a side, how would you figure out how many square units each area is?* [We want students to realize that they could fit 1-unit square tiles along the length. That line of tiles could be repeated over and over, each beside the previous line, covering the table. The number of repeats would be based on the width of the table; that is why the area is the length multiplied by the width.]

- *Why is it easier to figure out the area of a table top by using the length and width than by covering it with tiles?* [We want students to recognize why we appreciate formulas based on linear dimensions.]

- *What do you notice about the perimeters and areas of the tables?* [We want students to see that shapes with the same perimeter can have different areas.]

◆ **EXTENSION**   Ask students to sketch two rectangles with an area of 100 square inches that have different perimeters. Have them suggest how they might have predicted which has the greater perimeter. If students struggle, remind them why the length and width need to multiply to 100.

PERIMETER VERSUS AREA

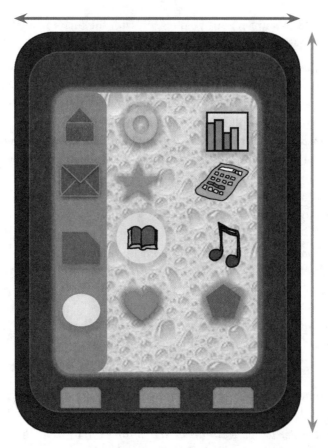

How can you use a ruler to estimate the perimeter?
How can you use a ruler to estimate the area?

❖ **MANY STUDENTS CONFUSE** area with perimeter. Many of them see both of these measures as describing how big a shape is and, in a way, they are correct. It becomes important, therefore, to distinguish between these two measures.

Questioning should bring out the difference between area and perimeter for a 2-D shape—that is, what each describes about the shape—and, in the case of the rectangle, how the length and width measures play into the calculation of each new measure. The difference between perimeter and area of a rectangle is first addressed in **Common Core State Standards 3.MD**.

The picture provided here is designed so that students see that a ruler can be used directly to estimate perimeter, but only indirectly to estimate area. In other words, one could take a string, wrap it around a shape and measure it against a ruler or one could move a ruler around the shape to estimate the perimeter. However, a ruler can only indirectly be used to measure area, using a formula either formally or informally.

❓ QUESTIONS to supplement the questions with the picture and to include in a conversation about the picture include

- *What kinds of measurements can a ruler give you?* [We want students to understand that rulers are used for linear measures, that is, lengths.]

- *What does perimeter mean?* [We want to ensure that students understand what we mean when we use the term "perimeter."]

- *Does every shape have a perimeter?* [We want students to generalize to realize any closed 2-D shape has a perimeter, even one with rounded corners. Even though we normally measure 3-D objects—for example, we measure a rectangle made of paper that is thin but does have a little bit of depth—flat objects can be considered as 2-D.]

- *How many numbers related to the shape did you use to estimate the perimeter?* [We want students to recognize that all side lengths of a rectangle are used to estimate the perimeter.]

- *Are there shapes where a different number of lengths are used to estimate the perimeter?* [We want students to associate the number of measures associated with perimeter to the number of sides of a shape.]

- *How would you usually estimate the area?* [We want students to recognize that they could tile the shape, although they might be ready to go right to the formula.]

- *Does the length affect the area? How? Does the width?* [We want students to recognize that both length and width affect the number of tiles that might be needed.]

- *Can you use a ruler to estimate the area? Explain.* [We want students to recognize that rulers can only be used in an indirect way (with a formula) and not directly to determine area.]

◆ EXTENSION   Ask students to draw a shape with a big perimeter and a relatively small area and a different shape with a big area and relatively small perimeter.

MEASUREMENT CONVERSIONS

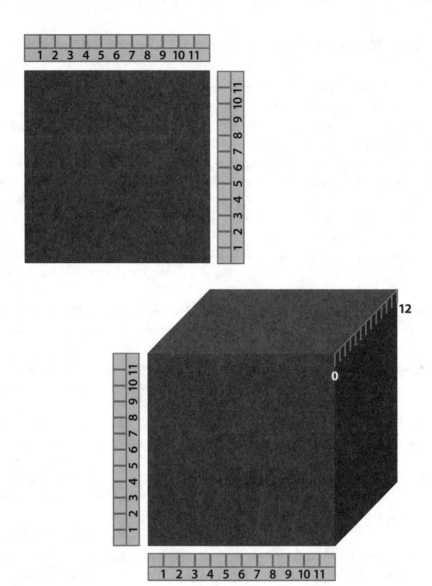

How many cubic inches would 10 cubic feet be?

❖ **SOMETIMES WE ARE** in a situation where we must compare measurements that are provided using different units. At other times we must use a tool that gives us a measurement in one unit (e.g., inches), but we cannot make sense of it until we think of it in terms of a more convenient unit (e.g., yards). In these situations, students need to

~~realize that knowing the relationship between two units can allow us to use calcula-~~ tions to represent a measurement provided one way in another way.

Questioning should bring out that knowing one conversion factor allows us to change any number of units of one type into units of another; for example, knowing that 12 inches = 1 foot means we also know that 24 inches = 2 feet, 120 inches = 10 feet, and 5 inches = $\frac{5}{12}$ of a foot. It is also important to bring out that conversions involving square or cubic units are different from conversions involving linear units; for example, since 12 inches = 1 foot, then 144 square inches = 1 square foot and 1728 cubic inches = 1 cubic foot. Measurement unit conversion is first addressed in **Common Core State Standards 4.MD**, where larger units are converted to smaller ones, and in **5.MD**, going the other way.

The picture provided here helps students to see why the conversion factors are squared or cubed in 2-D area and 3-D volume situations. They can see that 1 square foot is a 12-inch by 12-inch rectangle with an area of 12^2, or 144, square inches. They can also see that 1 cubic foot would have 12 layers of 1 square foot by 1 inch, and so the volume would be 12^3, or 1728 cubic inches.

? **QUESTIONS** to supplement the question with the picture and to include in a conversation about the picture include

- *Are there the same number of square inches in a square foot as inches in a foot? Why?* [We want students to recognize why conversion factors are squared or cubed in 2-D and 3-D situations.]

- *Suppose you knew the area of a shape in square feet. How would you figure out the area in square inches? Why?* [We want students to realize that you divide using the conversion factor to go from smaller units to bigger ones, but multiply to go from bigger units to smaller ones.]

- *Suppose you knew the area of a shape in square inches. How would you figure out the area in square feet? Why?*

- *Do you think there will be more or fewer cubic feet in a cubic yard than feet in a yard?* [We want students to generalize their thinking about inches and feet to other units.]

- *Do you think there will be more or fewer cubic feet in a cubic yard than cubic inches in a cubic foot? Why?* [We want students to realize that if we are converting when the linear conversion factor is smaller, the square and cubic conversion factors will also be smaller.]

- *When might you want to convert measurements?* [We want students to realize that this skill is valuable when comparing measures in different units or when a measure's value is too big or too small to make sense to us.]

◆ **EXTENSION**   Ask students to consider why they might use measurement conversions to decide whether a car with a 210 inch length is a long car or not.

GRAPHS WITH SCALES

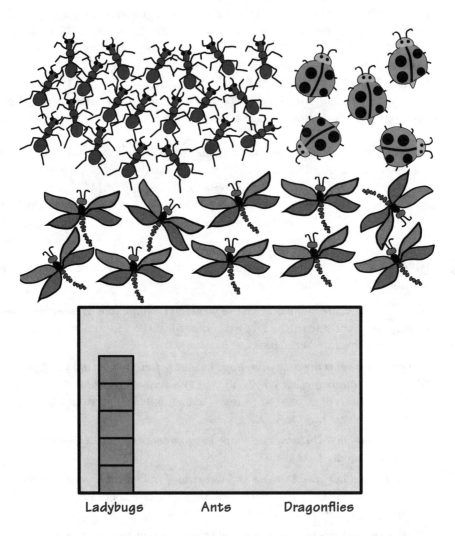

Ladybugs   Ants   Dragonflies

How can you change the graph to fit all of the information about the insects inside the green box?

▽ **ALTHOUGH EARLY EXPERIENCES** involving graphing do not require scales, once students attempt to graph data where frequencies are higher, there is a need for a scale. Otherwise, the bars for a bar graph or a line plot or the columns or rows of pictures in a picture graph are just too long or too wide to either fit the paper or interpret easily. It is only by having students confront the difficulty of representing data where the frequencies are high that this will become clear to them.

Questioning should bring out the notion that if any of the data involve a large number, a scale is probably useful. It should also bring out the notion that it is the size of the numbers as well as their values that could influence the choice of scale. For example, if a set of frequencies were 2, 8, 12, 14, and 10, a scale of 2 would make sense. But for frequencies such as 30, 45, 40, and 50, a scale of 5 or 10 would make more sense. The use of scale in graphing is first addressed in **Common Core State Standards 3.MD**.

The picture provided here is designed so that students see that a scale of 5 makes sense, although they might suggest a different scale. The ladybug frequency is graphed already, since that is not the information that would cause the dilemma. It is when students see that bar already created, and then have to figure out how to represent the other data within the green rectangle, that they realize something must change.

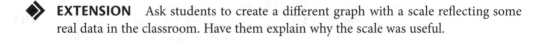

? QUESTIONS to supplement the question with the picture and to include in a conversation about the picture include

- *What does the red bar show?* [We want students to recognize that this is a bar graph about insect frequencies.]

- *Why would the bar for the ants be taller?* [We want to ensure that students recognize that the relative heights of bars reflect the relative frequencies of items.]

- *Suppose you started over and made every square represent five bugs. What would the graph look like?* [We want students to show understanding of how to use a scale.]

- *What other scale would have made sense?* [We want students to recognize that the scale used is a choice. For example, a scale of 2 or 10 might also have been used.]

- *Why is it useful to use a scale for a graph?* [We want students to recognize why scales are used.]

- *Would you have used a different scale if the numbers of bugs had been 4, 8, and 16?* [We want students to recognize that scales should reflect the data values.]

◆ EXTENSION   Ask students to create a different graph with a scale reflecting some real data in the classroom. Have them explain why the scale was useful.

COORDINATE GRIDS

Which monkey's tree is closer to the bananas?

 THE TOPIC OF COORDINATE GRIDS is an interesting one. Because grids describe location, there is an element of geometry attached to their use. But because they are so often used to describe relationships between two variables, they are usually associated with algebraic thinking.

What makes grids interesting, but also problematic, for some students is that although horizontal and vertical distances might be equal, diagonal distances are different. Some students struggle with this and suggest that each of the dark lines below represents a distance of 1 unit; in fact, if the horizontal and vertical distances each represent 1 unit, the other is more than 1 unit (actually about 1.4 units).

Questioning should address the fact that the first coordinate for a point on a grid tells the distance to the right of the origin and the second coordinate tells the distance up. The coordinate plane is first introduced in **Common Core State Standards 5.G**.

The picture with the monkeys is designed so that students realize that they must consider both horizontal and vertical distance from the origin in comparing distances. Although one tree is farther to the right, it is also lower down on the grid. Some students will compare the distances incorrectly by simply suggesting that both are 6 units from the bananas (4 squares over and 2 up or 1 square over and 5 up) (and will probably, and reasonably, think that they are supposed to be counting grid units since the grid is supplied). Some will count points rather than spaces. Some will want to duplicate the situation on grid paper and use a ruler to measure, which would give the correct answer that the rightmost tree is actually closer.

? QUESTIONS to supplement the question with the picture and to include in a conversation about the picture include

- *How many steps would you take to get to each tree?* [We want students to consider whether they would move "diagonally" or only horizontally and vertically.]

- *Why might someone think the trees are equally close to the bananas?*

- *What do you know about the lengths if you went directly in a line from the bananas to the base of each tree?* [We want students to notice the "triangles" that help define the distance to the origin.]

- *What coordinates could you use to describe each tree's position?* [We want students to show understanding of what each coordinate means.]

- *Do the coordinates actually tell you the distance the base of the tree is away from the bananas? The distance the monkey is from the bananas?* [We want students to realize that the distance is not either coordinate, nor their sum, but rather the directed distance, which turns out to be the square root of the sum of the squares of the coordinates (which does not have to be disclosed to students yet).]

◆ EXTENSION   Ask students where another monkey might be if it is the same distance from the bananas as one already on the grid. Have them explain how they know.

CLASSIFICATION OF SHAPES

People can have many names.

What different names
could you give this shape?

 AN IMPORTANT ASPECT of geometry is the recognition that some shapes are particular subsets of others. For example, a rectangle is a special case of a parallelogram, which is a special case of a quadrilateral, which is a special case of a polygon. This is a struggle for many, particularly, for example, for those who struggle to believe that a square is actually a rectangle.

The idea can be made clearer to students by recognizing that everything and everybody has lots of names. For example, a carrot is a vegetable and also a food. The notion of shape classification is addressed in **Common Core State Standards 5.G**.

The picture provided here is designed to make a connection to the fact that a person can have many names, depending on the audience. In a similar way, a shape can

138

have many names; the name we use depends on what properties of the shape we are addressing. If, for example, we are looking at a shape and only care whether the vertices form right angles, we might call a square a rectangle. But if we are interested in whether all the sides are equal, we would call the shape a square.

❓ QUESTIONS to supplement the question with the picture and to include in a conversation about the picture include

- *Why would different people call out differently to the person in the car?* [We want students to recognize that different names are about different relationships when we are talking about people.]

- *What is the first name you would give the shape?* [We want students to recognize that "square" is the most specialized name.]

- *Why might you call it a rectangle?* [We want to ensure that students realize that since any quadrilateral with four equal right angles is a rectangle, a square has to be a rectangle.]

- *Why might you just call it a polygon?* [We want students to realize that if the only thing we care about is whether the sides are straight, it is enough to call it a polygon.]

- *When might you want to be sure to call it a square?* [We want students to recognize that when we want to use certain measurement formulas that only apply to squares or when we want to know the relationship between the various side lengths we might use the term "square."]

- *What other shapes can you think of with different names?* [We want students to generalize this situation to other similar cases.]

- *Is it ever possible not to have two names?* [We want students to consider, thoughtfully, other possible situations. In fact, it would be difficult for students to think of such a situation; for example, even a circle could be called either a shape or a 2-D shape.]

◆ EXTENSION   Ask students to draw several different-looking shapes, each with three right angles. For each shape, they need to think of at least two (or more) possible names.

PARALLEL AND PERPENDICULAR LINES

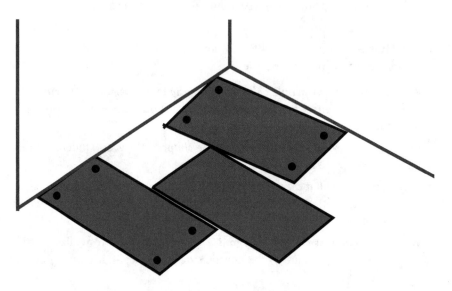

How can you be sure the floorboards are not parallel to each other?

❖ **STUDENTS OFTEN ASSOCIATE** parallelism and perpendicularity with properties of particular types of shapes. For example, all rectangles have both parallel and perpendicular sides, but parallelograms, more generally, might have only parallel sides. Or right triangles have perpendicular sides but not parallel sides. Although we want students to continue to make those associations of parallelism and perpendicularity with shapes, we want them to see that these ideas appear in their everyday lives as well.

One of the difficulties students have is that although they learn that parallel means that lines never meet, we cannot really ever test parallelism using that definition. None of us can draw a line "forever" to its full extent, so the question is how we know two lines do not meet somewhere far away. To do this, we need to use other properties of parallelism. One way to test whether two lines are parallel is to measure the perpendicular distance between them at three points and see if those values are all equal. Notice below that the distances are equal with the parallel lines but not with the nonparallel lines.

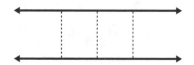
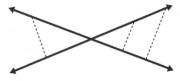

Another thing we can do is test whether a line that is perpendicular to one of the two presumed parallel lines is also perpendicular to the other. Recognition of parallelism and perpendicularity is addressed in **Common Core State Standards 4.G**.

The picture provided here is designed so that students see an example of a real-life use of parallelism and perpendicularity (getting the floor boards to fit) but also grasp the notion that you can test for parallelism by using perpendicularity.

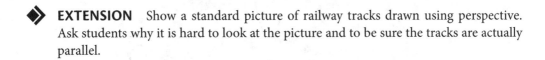

? QUESTIONS to supplement the question with the floorboard picture and include in a conversation about the picture include

- *How do you know which boards are perpendicular to the wall?* [We want students to know what perpendicularity means.]

- *How do you know which edges of the bottom left board are parallel?* [We want to ensure that students see how you can use a common perpendicular to test parallelism.]

- *How do you know that the middle board is not parallel to the top right one?* [We want students to recognize that parallelism requires maintaining a common distance.]

- *Why would you want floorboards to have parallel edges?* [We want students to recognize common uses of parallelism and perpendicularity.]

- *Why would you want floorboards laid perpendicular to a wall?*

◆ EXTENSION   Show a standard picture of railway tracks drawn using perspective. Ask students why it is hard to look at the picture and to be sure the tracks are actually parallel.

LINES OF SYMMETRY

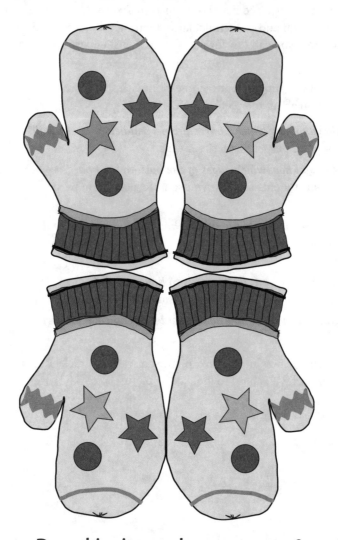

Does this picture show symmetry?

❖ **EVEN VERY YOUNG CHILDREN** are intuitively familiar with the concept of symmetry. Early picture books or experiences with people, blocks, toys, or games introduce them to the notion of symmetry. What may be new is the term "line of symmetry."

Questioning should bring out the notion that the line of symmetry could be a fold line or mirror line that divides the picture or shape into two mirror image halves. The discussion of line of symmetry is addressed in **Common Core State Standards 4.G**.

The picture provided here is designed to allow students to see that there can be more than one line of symmetry, but it is specifically designed to focus on the notion of shape versus color. When we think of line of symmetry from a mathematical point of view, it is the shape, not the color, that matters, although many students will reject that.

❓ QUESTIONS to supplement the question with the picture and to include in a conversation about the picture include

- *If the line of symmetry divides the picture into two identical halves in terms of shape (but not color), where would the line of symmetry be for this picture?* [We want students to know how to determine the line of symmetry.]

- *How could you prove it's a line of symmetry using folding?* [We want students to recognize that if you fold on the line of symmetry, one half of the image falls on top of the other half.]

- *How could you use a ruler to prove it's a line of symmetry?* [We want students to realize that matching objects are equally far from the line of symmetry.]

- *Why is there more than one option for the line of symmetry?* [We want students to realize that there is sometimes more than one line of symmetry.]

- *What do you notice about the two lines of symmetry?* [We want students to notice that the lines of symmetry intersect.]

◆ EXTENSION   Ask students to draw a different picture or shape where there are two lines of symmetry and to prove that both are lines of symmetry.

PATTERNS VERSUS NON-PATTERNS

Which would you call a pattern? Why?

❦ **WE SOMETIMES** take it for granted that students know what we mean by the term "pattern" and many do, but some might be less clear on the concept than we think. Students need to realize that we use the term "pattern" to connote predictability. It is not so much the numbers or the items that are used that make a pattern, but the arrangement of those numbers or items in a predictable way. Sometimes the predictability involves repetition of items, but often, as in the case in the top picture here, the predictability involves repetition of the amount of increase or decrease.

Questioning should bring out the notion of predictability being critical in the concept of pattern, but also that there might be alternate ways that the same items could be used in a predictable pattern. The notion of pattern as an element of algebraic thinking is first addressed in **Common Core State Standards 4.OA**.

The picture provided here is designed so that the very same items can be arranged in predictable or less predictable ways and to demonstrate that we only use the term "pattern" when there is predictability.

? **QUESTIONS** to supplement the questions with the picture and to include in a conversation about the picture include

- *Would you know how to continue the top picture? How would you do it?* [We want students to observe the predictability of the growing pattern and show that they can use that predictability to extend the pattern.]

- *Is there a different way to continue the top picture that makes sense to you?* [We want students to realize that until a "rule" is given, there are many ways to continue a pattern. For example: 2, 5, 8, 11 can be continued as 2, 5, 8, 11, 14, 17, . . . (add 3 each time) or as 2, 5, 8, 11, 15, 19, 23, 28, . . . (add 3 three times, then 4 three times, then 5 three times, etc.).]

- *Would you know how to continue the bottom picture? How would you do it?* [We want students to notice that if the items are not arranged in a predictable way, it is very hard to decide how to continue them. Some students will try to make a pattern out of what is not; this provides an opportunity to talk about how much we humans appreciate and seek predictability.]

- *Could you turn the bottom picture into a pattern?*

- *What makes something a pattern?* [We want students to explicitly articulate the notion that a pattern is about repetition or predictability.]

◆ **EXTENSION**   Ask students to use 20 tiles to start a pattern and explain how the pattern continues, and then to use exactly the same 20 tiles to create a non-pattern.

ALGEBRAIC THINKING: GROWING ADDITIVELY

At first, there were two bees.

More and more groups of three bees join them.

If this continues, what are some numbers of bees there could be and some numbers of bees there could not be?

 QUESTIONING FOR THIS PICTURE should focus on the fact that knowing how a pattern increases tells us, in broad strokes, what sorts of numbers can be in the pattern and what sorts of numbers cannot; this relates well to the notion of patterns being about predictability. The notion of growing patterns is first addressed in a significant way in **Common Core State Standards 4.OA**.

The picture provided here is designed so that the numbers of bees are not the multiples of 3 but are related to the multiples of 3 because they increase three at a time. We hope students will observe that numbers that are 1 less than a multiple of 3 can describe the total number of bees at any point in time, but no other numbers can. Some students might see this better using a table of values. Others might relate well to a simpler picture. A table is shown below; a simple picture appears on the next page.

Stage number	Number of bees
1	2
2	5
3	8
4	11

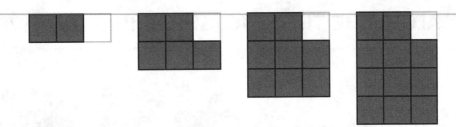

? **QUESTIONS** to supplement the question with the picture and to include in a conversation about the picture include

- *Could there ever be 21 bees? Explain.* [We want students to notice that since we did not begin with a multiple of 3 bees, if we keep adding 3s, we will never get to a multiple of 3.]

- *What number close to 33 bees might there be?* [We want students to begin to notice that the numbers are each 1 less than a multiple of 3.]

- *Why can't there be exactly 100 bees at any one time?*

- *How close to 100 might there be? Why that number?*

- *What is a big number of bees there might eventually be?* [We want students to apply what they noticed about smaller numbers to larger numbers. They must create a number 1 less than a multiple of 3 that is fairly large, for example, 2999.]

- *What is a big number of bees there could not be?* [We want students to apply what they noticed about smaller numbers to larger numbers. They could choose a multiple of 3, such as 6000, or a number 1 more than a multiple of 3, such as 9901.]

- *How far apart are the numbers that describe the total number of bees at any particular time?* [We want students to observe that because the pattern increases by 3, numbers in the pattern are a multiple of 3 apart.]

◆ **EXTENSION**   Ask students to create several patterns where the number of items in a part of the pattern could be 50 or 80, but not 60 or 70.

ALGEBRAIC THINKING: SHRINKING ADDITIVELY

How many birds might be left after a lot of pairs leave?

❖ **JUST AS STUDYING PATTERNS** that increase can build number sense, so can studying patterns that decrease.

Questioning in this case should focus on the fact that figuring out the possible number of birds can be accomplished by thinking about a pattern and knowing that how a pattern decreases tells us what sorts of numbers can be in the pattern and what sorts of numbers cannot. As with patterns that increase, examination of what numbers are possible and what ones are not relates well to the notion of patterns being about predictability. The concept of shrinking patterns is first addressed in a significant way in **Common Core State Standards 4.OA**.

The picture provided here is designed so that the numbers of birds is always an even number since the initial number is even and the birds leave in pairs. Students will likely need to do some mental rearranging to see that there are 50 birds to start with, because the numbers on the wires are not 10, 10, 10, 10, and 10, but 9, 10, 11, 11, and 9.

? **QUESTIONS** to supplement the question with the picture and to include in a conversation about the picture include

- *How do you know that the numbers are all less than 50?* [We want students to observe that the values in a pattern can decrease.]

- *Is it easy to predict how many there will be after 20 pairs leave?* [We want students to have a method for calculating the possible numbers.]

- *Could there ever be 25 birds left? Explain.*

- *What other numbers could be left?* [We want students to see that they are actually examining the pattern 50, 48, 46, 44, 42, 40, 38, ...]

- *What numbers less than 50 could not be left?* [We want students to see that these values also form a pattern: 49, 47, 45, 43, ... Some students will suggest that fractions or even negative numbers cannot be left and this, of course, is also true.]

- *Suppose you want it to be possible that there are 25 birds left, but the birds still fly off in pairs. How many birds would you want there to be at the start?* [We want students to realize that the initial value must be odd if decreasing by 2 each time leaves an odd number in the pattern.]

◆◆ **EXTENSION**   Ask students to create several bird patterns where the number of birds left could be 22 or 47, but not 10.

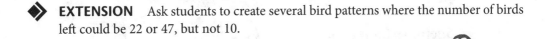

ALGEBRAIC THINKING:
GROWING MULTIPLICATIVELY

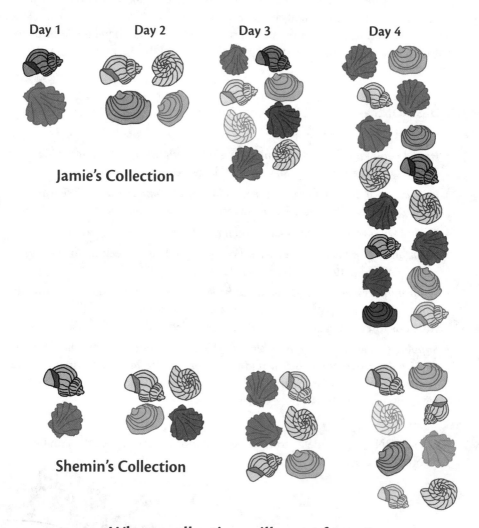

Day 1   Day 2   Day 3   Day 4

Jamie's Collection

Shemin's Collection

Whose collection will grow faster?

❖ **ALTHOUGH MOST OF THE PATTERNS** that students in this grade band explore are patterns that increase or decrease by the same amount all the time, there are natural circumstances where patterns are based on doubling, tripling, etc. These sorts of patterns become more important in later grades, but students in this grade band are certainly able to see how much more quickly multiplicative patterns grow (assuming a whole number multiplier) than patterns based on adding.

Questioning should focus on the relative rates of growth of the two patterns, one multiplicative and one additive. The concept of comparing these types of patterns is first addressed in a significant way in **Common Core State Standards 5.OA**.

The picture provided here is designed so that students are comparing corresponding terms of two relevant patterns; this is done by using day designations as a way to match items in the two patterns. Students will see that even though the numbers of shells initially are the same, very soon it is Jamie's amounts that are much greater than Shemin's.

? **QUESTIONS** to supplement the question with the picture and to include in a conversation about the picture include

- *Can you predict how many shells each will have on Day 5?* [We want students to use what they observe about a pattern to extend it.]

- *Will Shemin ever have more shells than Jamie?* [We want students to recognize that once Jamie's number of shells surpasses Shemin's, it will never go back.]

- *Why does Jamie usually, but not always, gain more shells from day to day?* [We want students to observe that doubling an amount more than 2 increases it much more than adding 2 to it.]

◆ **EXTENSION**   Ask students to compare a pattern that begins at 1 and where each new term is double the previous term to a pattern that begins at 200 and where each new term is 2 more than the previous term. We want them to see that even in this more extreme case, eventually the doubling pattern will overtake the one based on adding.

CHAPTER 4

Grades 6–8

COMMON FACTORS

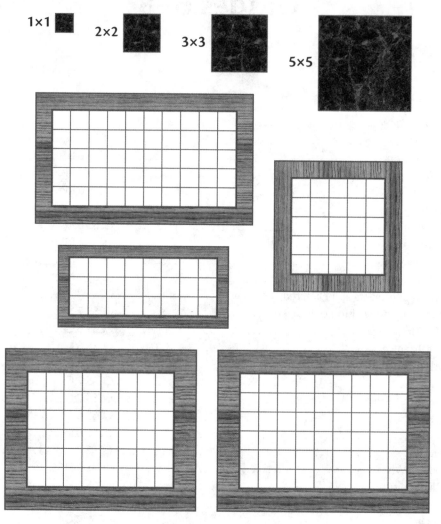

Which tiles can be used (without cutting) to perfectly fit each of these rectangle frames?

⩔ **TO SIMPLIFY FRACTIONS** and to solve certain types of problems, students need to know about common factors. For example, it is useful to know that 3 is a common factor of 6 and 9 when writing the fraction $\frac{6}{9}$ as the simpler equivalent $\frac{2}{3}$. It is also useful to know that 3 is a common factor of 6 and 9 when trying to determine what size tile could be used, without cutting any tiles, to cover an area that is 6 units wide by 9 units long.

Students learn to determine common factors either by guessing and testing or by factoring each number and looking for factors the numbers have in common. Students should be aware that 1 is always a common factor of any two numbers and that any common factor is less than or equal to the lesser of the two numbers being factored. The topic of common factors is addressed in **Common Core State Standards 6.NS**.

The picture provided here is designed to focus students on the notion that square tiles of different sizes can often exactly fit rectangular spaces, but the tile edge lengths are limited to those that are factors of both the length and the width, if the tiles are not to be cut.

❓ QUESTIONS to supplement the question with the picture and to include in a conversation about the picture include

* *Which tiles can you use for the 6 × 8 picture? Why?* [We want students to notice that a tile with a linear dimension of 3 or 5 will not work because neither dimension is a factor of both 6 and 8.]

* *Which tiles can you use for the 6 × 9 picture? Why?* [We want students to notice that a tile with a linear dimension of 1 or 3 will work because either dimension is a factor of both numbers, but a 2 × 2 tile will not work because 2 is a factor of 6 but not of 9.]

* *In which frames will the 5 × 5 tile fit? Explain.* [We want students to realize that the only possibility is one where both dimensions are multiples of 5, namely 5 × 5 or 5 × 10 in the picture provided.]

* *Which tile always works? Why?* [We want students to recognize that 1 is a factor of every whole number.]

* *In which other sizes of frames, not in the picture, would the 3 × 3 tile fit?* [We want students to recognize that there is an infinite number of possibilities that can be found by using many different multiples of 3 as lengths and widths.]

◆ EXTENSION   Present the following problem: Classes of two different sizes were each divided into the same number of groups. No students were left out in either class. The group sizes were the same in each class, but different from one class to the next. First ask students how big the classes might have been and how many groups were in each. Then ask how this problem is like the tile problem. The objective is for students to see that this is another common factor problem since both classes had a common group size.

COMMON MULTIPLES

Hot dogs come in
packages of 6

Hot dog buns come in
packages of 8

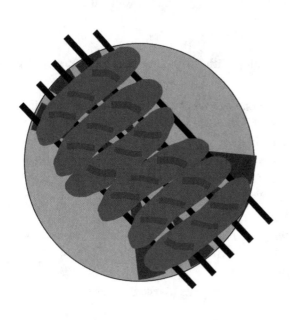

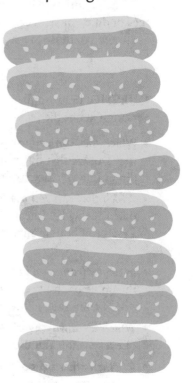

How many packages of buns and packages of hot dogs would you need to buy to have a bun for each dog and none left over?

❖ **STUDENTS USE COMMON MULTIPLES** both to determine common denominators for computations with fractions (e.g., adding, subtracting, or possibly dividing fractions) and to solve certain types of problems.

One way to calculate common multiples is to factor each number into primes and use as few of each required prime as possible. In the hot dog/bun example, students might recognize that they need a common multiple of 6 and 8. They might just know that 24 works, or they might factor hot dogs and buns as follows:

$$6 = 3 \times 2$$
$$8 = 2 \times 2 \times 2$$

Thus, the least common multiple is made up of three 2s (since 8 has three 2s, even though 6 has only one) and one 3 (since 6 has one 3, even though 8 has none). We want students to recognize that each common multiple is at least as great as the greater of the two numbers, and that there is an infinite number of common multiples. The topic of common multiples is first addressed in **Common Core State Standards 6.NS**.

The picture provided here is designed to help students recognize when a common multiple is useful for solving a problem.

? **QUESTIONS** to supplement the question with the picture and to include in a conversation about the picture include

- *Why can't you buy exactly 12 hot dog buns?* [We want students to realize that you can only buy multiples of 8 buns in this situation.]
- *How do you know which numbers of hot dog buns you could buy?*
- *Why can't you buy exactly 16 hot dogs?* [We want students to realize that you can only buy multiples of 6 hot dogs in this situation.]
- *How do you know which numbers of hot dogs you could buy?*
- *Why are there a lot of possible answers to the question with the picture?* [We want students to realize that as soon as you calculate one common multiple, you can multiply it by any whole number at all to get another common multiple.]
- *What do you notice about the numbers of packages of buns and hot dogs?* [We want students to notice that the number of packages of buns is always a multiple of 3 (to ensure that the total number of buns is a multiple of 6) and that the number of packages of hot dogs is always a multiple of 4 (to ensure that the total number of hot dogs is a multiple of 8).]

◆▷ EXTENSION Present the following problem: Ellen works at a shelter every 10th day and Lisa works there every 6th day. If they both work there today, how many days will it be before they work together again? Ask how this problem is related to the problem of the hot dogs and buns. Students should realize that it would have to be the 20th, 30th, 40th, . . . day (multiples of 10) for Ellen to be at the shelter and would have to be the 12th, 18th, 24th, . . . day (multiples of 6) for Lisa to be at the shelter. Clearly, a common multiple is required.

SQUARE ROOTS

17 square yards

**If the field is square,
how do you know how wide it is?**

ALTHOUGH STUDENTS MIGHT associate the term square root with a strictly numerical situation—defining it as the number to multiply by itself to achieve a given product—it is important for them to have a geometric sense of what square root is, as well. The square root of a number can be thought of as the side length of a square when its area is that number. For example, the square root of 25 is 5, since a square that has a side length of 5 units has an area of 25 square units.

Although students often can make sense of square roots of certain numbers—such as 25, 36, 49, etc. (numbers that are perfect squares)—it is valuable that they extend this thinking to other numbers that are not perfect squares. The topic of square root is first addressed in **Common Core State Standards 8.EE**. The image here is best used *prior to* introduction of the definition of square root.

The picture provided is set up to help students make the numerical/geometric connection between the square root of 16 being 4 and the square root of 17 being slightly more than 4.

❓ QUESTIONS to supplement the question with the picture and to include in a conversation about the picture include

- *How do you know that the side length is less than 5 units?* [We want students to use benchmarks to estimate the side length, or the square root of 17.]

- *What else do you know about the side length?* [We want students to take the opportunity to share what they can infer from the picture.]

- *How do you know if the side length is closer to 4 than to 5?* [We want students to consider two benchmarks simultaneously.]

- *How could you use grid paper to estimate the side length to the nearest tenth of a unit?* [We want students to extend their thinking to be more precise. They might, for example, draw a picture like the one below to estimate the square root as 4.1.]

- *How could you prove your estimate is reasonable?* [We want them to realize you can multiply the square root by itself to relate squaring to taking the square root.]

◆ EXTENSION   Ask students to draw a picture that would help them estimate $\sqrt{34}$. Students could begin with a 5 × 5 grid and extend both the length and the width in such a way to produce a total of about 9 extra units of area. That would involve almost 0.9 additional units of length and width.

FRACTION DIVISION

FLOUR

$3\frac{1}{2}$ cups

$\frac{1}{3}$ cup

What number sentence would you use to figure out how many times to fill the scoop to measure all of the flour?

❖ **THE MEANING OF DIVISION** is no different when dividing fractions than it is when dividing whole numbers. Students need to recognize that $a \div b$ always asks how many bs are in a. For example, $2 \div \frac{1}{2}$ asks how many halves are in 2.

When the answer is not a whole number, students need to relate the "remainder" to the divisor. For example, $2\frac{1}{4} \div \frac{1}{2} = 4\frac{1}{2}$, not $4\frac{1}{4}$. This is because there are 4 groups of $\frac{1}{2}$ in the 2 part, but there is only $\frac{1}{2}$ of a $\frac{1}{2}$ in the $\frac{1}{4}$ part. The topic of dividing fractions is first addressed in **Common Core State Standards 6.NS**.

The picture provided here is set up to help students recognize how dividing of fractions works and how to deal with the remainder when the last $\frac{1}{3}$ cup has been used and there is still some flour left.

❓ **QUESTIONS** to supplement the question with the picture and to include in a conversation about the picture include

- *How do you know the number of fills of the measuring scoop is more than 9?*
  [We want students to estimate using a related simpler calculation, i.e., $3 \div \frac{1}{3}$.]

- *How do you know the number of fills of the measuring scoop is more than 10?* [We want students to estimate more closely.]

- *How full is the measuring scoop for the last bit? How do you know?* [We want students to think about the ratio of the remainder of the flour to the size of the measuring scoop.]

- *What operation did you use in your number sentence? Why that one?* [We want students to relate counting the number of groups to division (or possibly multiplication).]

- *Why is the quotient $10\frac{1}{3}$ and not $10\frac{1}{6}$?* [We want students to realize that the answer must be related to the divisor and not a full 1 cup unit.]

- *How would your answer change if you had to measure $3\frac{3}{4}$ cups of flour?* [We want students to relate the new calculation to a previously completed one.]

- *How would your answer change if you had to measure $3\frac{1}{3}$ cups of flour with a $\frac{1}{2}$ cup measuring device?* [We want to give students another problem to try, with the opportunity to relate it to the previously solved problem.]

 EXTENSION   Ask students to create several other fraction division problems with the same answer as the problem in the picture here. This could help them realize that if you double the amount of flour and double the measuring scoop size, nothing changes, or more generally, that you can multiply both the dividend and divisor by any factor, as long as the factor is the same for both.

RATIOS: MULTIPLE RATIOS DESCRIBE ANY SITUATION

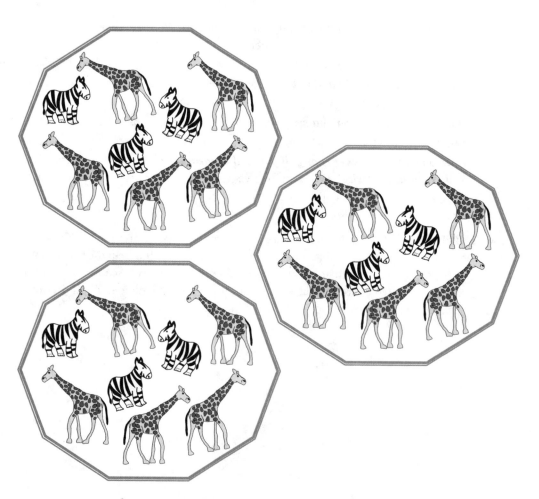

What comparisons does the picture show?

❖ **RATIO SITUATIONS** can usually be described in the form "*m* of one type of item for every *n* of another type." But within each of these situations, there are always at least three more ratios. For example, if there are 10 boys playing intramurals for each 6 girls playing intramurals, we can write 10 boys:6 girls, but we can also write 6 girls:10 boys, 10 boys:16 students, or 6 girls:16 players.

When the number of boys is compared to the number of girls, we call it a "part-to-part ratio," since parts of a whole are being compared. When either the number of boys or the number of girls is compared to the total number of players, we call it a "part-to-whole ratio." We want students to realize that if the ratio of type *a*:type *b* is *a*:*b*, then the number of items of type *a* is a multiple of *a*, the number of items of type *b* is the same multiple of *b*, and the number of total items is the same multiple of (*a* + *b*). Ratio is first explicitly addressed in **Common Core State Standards 6.RP**.

The picture provided here is set up to help students recognize that the giraffes could be compared to the zebras or each type of animal could be compared to the whole group of animals. The animals are set up in 3 groups to make it clear that it is not just that there are 9 zebras and 15 giraffes, but that there are always 3 zebras for each 5 giraffes.

? **QUESTIONS** to supplement the question with the picture and to include in a conversation about the picture include

- *What does the ratio 3:8 tell about the animals?* [We want students to attend to the different ratios associated with the picture and tell what each one describes.]

- *What does the ratio 3:5 tell about the animals?*

- *How would knowing that the ratio of zebras to giraffes is 3:5 tell you that fewer than half the animals are zebras?* [We want students to recognize that the part-to-whole ratio would be 3:8, which is less than half, 4:8.]

- *If the ratio of zebras to giraffes had been 4:3 instead, what would you know about the picture?* [We want students to infer as much information as possible from a given ratio. For example, they might realize that more than half the animals are zebras, that the number of zebras is a multiple of 4, that the total number of animals is a multiple of 7, etc.]

◆ **EXTENSION**   Ask students to draw a picture that shows both the ratios 4:11 and 7:11 at the same time. Then ask what other ratios their picture shows. Ideally, they will realize that they need to create a picture of groups of 11 items where there are 4 of one type and 7 of another type in each group.

EQUIVALENT RATIOS

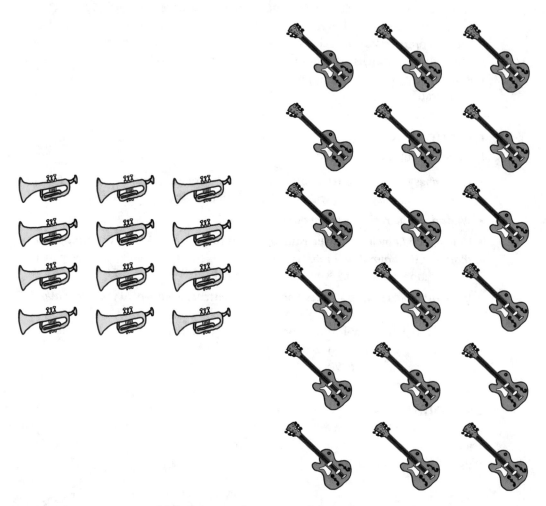

What numbers could you use
in the blanks to describe the picture?
_____ of every _____ are guitars.

⧩ **BECAUSE RATIOS ARE NOT ABSOLUTE**, but comparative, there are many ways to describe the comparison. For example, if there are 2 red counters for every 3 blue ones, there are also 4 reds for every 6 blue, 6 reds for every 9 blue, etc. These forms of the same comparison are called equivalent ratios. In fact, both terms of the ratio can be multiplied or divided by any non-zero amount to get an equivalent ratio, but *adding* to both terms does not generally produce an equivalent ratio.

It is important for students to become comfortable with the concept of equivalent ratios in order to solve ratio, rate, and percent problems. For example, if you know that 2 cups of flour is used to make 12 cookies, and you want to know how much flour you would need to make 20 cookies, you need to find a ratio equivalent to 2:12 where the second term is 20. Equivalent ratios are first explicitly addressed in **Common Core State Standards 6.RP**.

The picture of trumpets and guitars provided here is set up to help students see some of those equivalences immediately, although they could extrapolate to come up with other ideas.

? QUESTIONS to supplement the question with the picture and to include in a conversation about the picture include

- *What is true about every group of 10 instruments in the picture? How would you write this as a ratio?* [We want students to address one form of the ratio, for example, 6:10 or 4:10 in this case, and to use standard ratio notation.]

- *What is a simpler way to describe that ratio? Why is it simpler?* [We want students to recognize that there is always a simplest form of a ratio.]

- *What is true about 3 out of every 5? How would you write this as a ratio?*

- *Could you write 24 out of every 60 to describe this picture?* [We want students to use equivalent ratios beyond what is visible in the picture. One is somewhat more obvious than the other.]

- *How could you generate other ratios to describe the picture? How many would there be?* [We want students to realize that there is an infinite number of equivalent ratios. We can simply keep doubling both terms of the ratio.]

- *How would it be useful to use an equivalent ratio to solve the following problem: Suppose there were 48 trumpets. How many guitars would there be?* [We want students to see the value of using equivalent ratios. In this case, it would be the equivalent 48:72 (equivalent to 2:3).]

- *Why can you multiply both terms of a ratio to get an equivalent one, but not add to both terms?* [We want to emphasize that ratios are always multiplicative comparisons.]

◆ EXTENSION   Ask students which of these numbers they could use to make pairs of equivalent ratios: 4, 5, 6, 9, 10, 15, 20, 24, 36, 40, 45, 60, 100. Hopefully they use number sense to help. For example, they might notice that 4:5 = 36:45 and that 9:24 = 15:40.

EQUIVALENT RATES

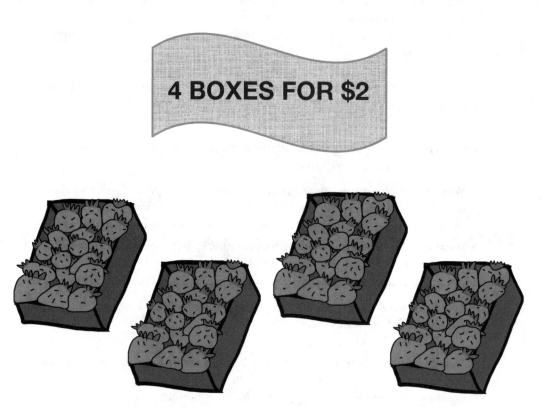

4 BOXES FOR $2

Why might someone describe the price by saying the berries cost 50¢ a box, while someone else would say you can buy 2 boxes for $1?

◆ **JUST AS WITH RATIOS**, there are always multiple ways to describe the same rate. For example, if you are driving 50 km/hour, the speed can also be described as 5 km/6 minutes, 25 km/30 minutes, 100 km/2 hours, etc. As with ratios, each term in the rate is multiplied or divided by exactly the same amount, other than 0. It is important that students realize that both terms are multiplied (or divided) and that adding and subtracting are not appropriate.

One particularly useful type of equivalent rate is what is called the "unit rate." In this case, the rate is expressed so that either the second term or the first term is 1. For example, 50 km/1 hour is a unit rate, but so is 1.2 minutes/1 km (in this case, each term is divided by 50, after 1 hour is converted to 60 minutes).

Because many real-life problems are solved by using equivalent rates, it is important for students to become comfortable with the concept. For example, if we want to know how long it takes a heart to beat 1000 times if it beats 72 beats/minute, we need to determine an equivalent to the rate 72 beats/1 minute with a first term of 1000 beats. Equivalent ratios/rates are first explicitly addressed in **Common Core State Standards 6.RP**.

The picture provided here is designed to focus students on the alternate ways that unit rates can be written. In the first instance, a price for 1 box is given, but in the second instance, the number of boxes for $1 is given; other equivalent rates might also be introduced.

? **QUESTIONS** to supplement the question with the picture and to include in a conversation about the picture include

- *Why do you think a rate might be given in terms of the cost of 2 boxes instead of just 1 box?* [We want students to consider why a particular form of a rate might be used. Students can use real-life experience to answer.]

- *How much would 8 boxes cost? How else could the price have been advertised using that information?* [We want students to recognize that an equivalent rate is a fair description of the given rate.]

- *Which of the ways to describe the price in the question do you think is a better way? Why?* [We want students to be able to compare two forms of a rate and decide the circumstances in which each might be best.]

- *Is there always more than one way to describe a price? Explain.* [We want students to recognize that there is always an infinite number of equivalent rates that can be used.]

◆ **EXTENSION**   Ask students to do some research to determine some typical rates (e.g., related to the environment, to entertainment, to biology, etc.) and express those rates in a variety of ways, including as a unit rate in more than one way. Examples of such rates include batting averages in baseball, pollution rates, and costs of waste removal in a city.

SOLVING RATE PROBLEMS

I have gone 12 km in the last 40 minutes.

What calculations could you use to describe Andrea's speed? Which of those descriptions is most meaningful?

THE IDEAS ADDRESSED in this visual are important. We want students to use their number sense to relate rates without always calculating a unit rate. For example, one of the places we use rates is to describe prices. A student should know that 2 boxes for $8 is more expensive than 4 boxes for $15 without actually determining what one box costs. It is also important for students to relate the type of calculations they use to determine a missing term in an equivalent rate to a mathematical operation. For example, to determine the cost of 6 cookies if we know that 5 cost $8, we must either multiply 8 by $\frac{6}{5}$ or divide 8 by $\frac{5}{6}$. Solving rate problems is explicitly addressed in **Common Core State Standards 6.RP**.

The picture provided here is designed to give students the opportunity to use equivalent rates to describe a speed and to consider which description or representation of that speed is most meaningful and how it was calculated.

?   **QUESTIONS** to supplement the questions with the picture and to include in a conversation about the picture include

- *How do you know Andrea's speed was more than 12 km per hour?* [We want students to use fraction/ratio number sense to know that 12 km in 40 minutes is clearly faster than 12 km in 1 hour.]

- *How do you know it's less than 24 km per hour?* [We want students to use fraction/ratio number sense to know that 24 km per hour is the same as 12 km per half hour; that's faster than 12 km in 40 minutes.]

- *Would it be useful to describe her speed as so many kilometers per 10 minutes? Would it be easy to do?* [We want students to recognize that there could be merit in going from 40 minutes to 10 minutes, since then it would be easy to calculate kilometers per hour.]

- *What calculations could you do with fractions to figure out her speed in kilometers per hour?* [We want students to realize that to determine kilometers per hour, we could either divide by $\frac{2}{3}$ or multiply by $\frac{3}{2}$.]

- *Why would that calculation make sense?* [We want students to think about dividing by $\frac{2}{3}$ as calculating a unit rate and multiplying by $\frac{3}{2}$ as recognizing that 60 is $1\frac{1}{2}$ times as much as 40.]

◆   **EXTENSION**   Ask students to set up rate problems that could be solved using each of these calculations: $40 \div \frac{3}{5}$ and $20 \times \frac{4}{3}$. *Examples:* If 3 days of car rental cost $40, how much should 5 cost at the same rate? If 3 boxes of detergent cost $20, how much should 4 boxes cost?

DESCRIBING PERCENT

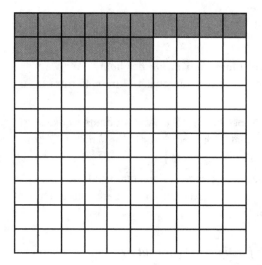
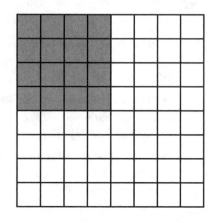
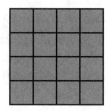

Which grid or grids show percent?

❖ **THIS VISUAL IS DESIGNED** to bring out the important idea that percent can be used to describe any part of a whole, whether the whole is made up of 100 parts or not. However, students need to realize that if there are not 100 parts, they need to do some calculation to figure out what percent they are looking at. Sometimes these calculations are relatively simple (e.g., if the grid has 50 parts) and sometimes they are much more complex (e.g., if the grid has 38 parts). The notion that percent is a ratio, or a fraction, can also easily be addressed using this approach. Percent is introduced in **Common Core State Standards 6.RP**.

The picture has one grid with 100 squares, making the percent very easy to identify; a second grid with one quarter shaded, so it can be related to the commonly understood 25%; and a third grid fully shaded, so that students can appreciate the notion that a whole is always 100%, whatever that whole is.

? **QUESTIONS** to supplement the question with the picture and to include in a conversation about the picture include

- *What does percent mean?* [We want to ensure that students know the definition of percent.]

- *Which grid is easiest to describe with percent? Why?* [We want students to recognize that 100% is easy to see no matter what the grid size and that grid sizes of 100 are also easy to describe with percent.]

- *Suppose half of a grid is shaded. Would the grid size matter if you were describing what percent is shaded? Why or why not?* [We want students to recognize that the fraction $\frac{1}{2}$ is synonymous with 50% no matter what the whole is.]

- *What size grids would be easiest to describe in terms of percent? Which would be more difficult? Why?* [We want students to realize that a grid with a factor of 100 as the number of squares might be easiest to describe with percents. But some students will realize that any size grid is easy to use with 100%, 0%, or possibly 50%.]

- *Is a percent a ratio? Is it a fraction?* [We want students to know that any percent is a ratio with a second term of 100, or a fraction with a denominator of 100.]

◆◆ **EXTENSION**   Ask students to shade 6 squares in each of these grids and describe the percent shaded:

- A grid with 200 squares (3%)
- A grid with 50 squares (12%)
- A grid with 500 squares (1.2%)
- A grid with 150 squares (4%)

USES OF INTEGERS

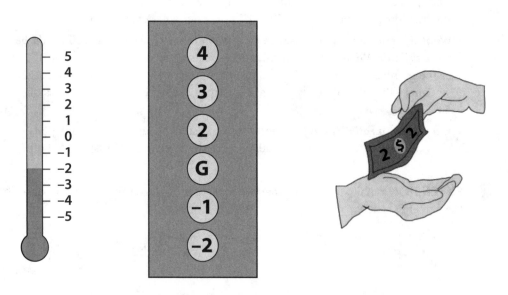

In which real-life situations might it make sense to use integers?

⯆ **INTEGERS INCLUDE** all the whole numbers and their opposites on the number line. Becoming comfortable with integers is a critical prerequisite to secondary mathematics. The problem is that integers are not "real." There is no actual –1. Instead, negative integers are abstractions; the definition of –1 is the number you add to 1 to get 0. This becomes particularly difficult for students when an integer is modeled as, for example, a counter of certain color, which, on the surface, looks as much like +1 as a counter of a different color.

One of the models typically used for integers is a number line, either horizontal or vertical. This model is probably the one that helps students best understand why negative numbers are less than positive ones. However, negative numbers are used in other contexts, with which students should become familiar. Integers are introduced in **Common Core State Standards 6.NS**.

The picture suggests a number of contexts in which negative numbers make sense. It provides the opportunity for students to consider how these various uses of negative numbers can be related.

? QUESTIONS to supplement the question with the picture and to include in a conversation about the picture include

- *What ideas do the pictures give you for meanings for –2?* [We want students to make connections between the situations presented and the number –2.]

- *What other situations can you think of where –2 would be meaningful?* [We want students to describe their own personal connections with negative numbers.]

- *What does the 2 tell you about –2? What does the – tell you?* [We want students to recognize the relative size and position of –2 by placing it on the number line.]

- *What side of the line is –2 on? Why?*

- *Why do you think –2 is called the opposite of +2?* [We want students to make a connection between the placement of positive and negative integers.]

- *What other things can you say about –2?* [We want students to realize that there are many other things to be said about any number. For example, we can say that –2 is less than 0, less than 10, more than –3, closer to 0 than –12, etc.]

◆ EXTENSION Ask students which of the models shown in the visual they think would be most useful to explain why –12 is less than –2, and why they chose those models. For example, some students might choose money because money is something "real" and they can relate to it more readily, but others might choose either the number line, the thermometer, or the elevator panel since those items show how far –12 is below –2.

THE ZERO PRINCIPLE

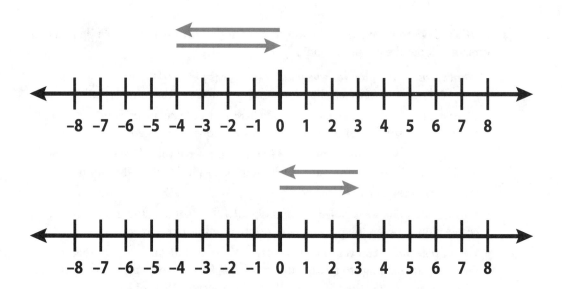

What do all of these pictures show?

◈ **A VITAL ASPECT** of making sense of addition and subtraction of integers, and to a certain extent multiplication and division, is a fulsome understanding of the notion that "the sum of a negative integer and its opposite" is another name for 0. Often students use a model of positive (+1) and negative (−1) counters. Therefore, 4 + (−2) is modeled as:

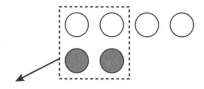

In this picture, white counters represent +1, dark counters represent –1, and the dashed box and arrow shows that combinations of +1 and –1, which make 0s, can be eliminated without changing the value of what is present. The sum is clearly +2.

Similarly, to model 4 – (–2), we can start with 4 positive (white) counters. We want to take away 2 negative (dark) counters, but there are none. However, without changing our original 4, we can add 0 twice by introducing 2 positive and 2 negative counters. Then the 2 negative counters can be removed to perform our original operation of subtracting –2 (as indicated by the solid box and arrow). The result is 6 positive counters remaining, or +6.

Add zero twice

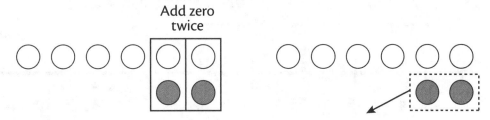

The zero principle is introduced in **Common Core State Standards 7.NS**.

The number lines in the picture provided here provide yet another model of the zero principle. In this model, an arrow on a number line going in one direction "undoes" an arrow going in the other direction; going backward undoes going forward.

? QUESTIONS to supplement the question with the picture and to include in a conversation about the picture include

- *How else can you get to 0 on a number line using two moves? How would you write these as number sentences?* [We want students to realize that the sentence is always either of the form $n – n = 0$ or $n + (– n) = 0$. These both really say the same thing.]

- *What is true in every instance so far?* [We want students to observe that a number is always added to its opposite.]

- *How are the counters in the picture like the number lines?* [We want students to make the connection between matching a number to its opposite in the two situations.]

- *These pictures are all examples of the zero principle. What do you think the zero principle says?* [We want students to explicitly articulate the principle that a number added to its opposite is 0.]

◆ EXTENSION   Ask students what other pictures they could think of to show the zero principle. They might, for example, consider adding debts to assets of the same amount or think about temperatures rising and falling the same amount.

SUBTRACTION OF INTEGERS AS A DIRECTED DISTANCE

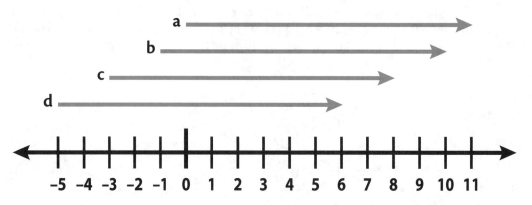

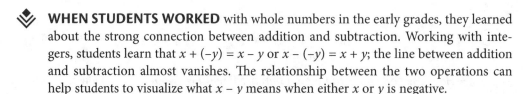

Do these arrows show addition or subtraction?
What do you notice each time?

WHEN STUDENTS WORKED with whole numbers in the early grades, they learned about the strong connection between addition and subtraction. Working with integers, students learn that $x + (-y) = x - y$ or $x - (-y) = x + y$; the line between addition and subtraction almost vanishes. The relationship between the two operations can help students to visualize what $x - y$ means when either x or y is negative.

We want students to recognize that no matter whether working with positives or negatives, $x - y$ is the directed distance from y to x. For example, to model 5 – 3, we want to know what to add to 3 to get 5, so we start at 3 and count the number of spaces to 5. Similarly, –5 – 3 = –8 should tell what to add to 3 to get to –5. Since the distance from 3 to –5 is 8 in the negative direction, an answer of –8 makes sense. In the picture provided, the arrows show 11 – 0 or 0 + 11 (arrow a), 10 – (–1) or –1 + 11 (arrow b), 8 – (–3) or –3 + 11 (arrow c), and 6 – (–5) or –5 + 11 (arrow d). Subtraction of integers is introduced in **Common Core State Standards 7.NS**.

The picture provided here builds on the number line model for subtracting integers and not only shows how addition and subtraction of integers are related, but also that another way to calculate, for example, 8 – (–3) (i.e., the distance from –3 to 8), is to shift that operation up to numbers that are more comfortable to subtract, such as 11 – 0.

? **QUESTIONS** to supplement the questions with the picture and to include in a conversation about the picture include

- *What number sentence could each arrow be describing?* [We want students to recognize that each arrow can be thought of as adding 11 to some number or as a model for a subtraction indicating how much farther to the right one number is than another.]

- *Why might the number sentence to describe each arrow be either an addition or a subtraction?* [We want students to realize that addition and subtraction sentences are always interrelated.]

- *Do the pictures show take-away subtraction or some other kind of subtraction? What kind?* [We want students to relate subtraction to a missing addend.]

- *What "story" might each arrow be mathematizing?* [We want students to relate the mathematical operation to an actual situation, for example, a temperature rise or fall.]

- *How do your number sentences make sense of the fact that all the arrows shown are the same length?* [We want students to observe that the difference is the same when both the minuend and subtrahend are increased by the same amount. This shows up by having the same missing addend each time or the same difference each time.]

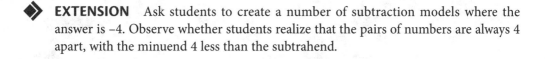

◆ **EXTENSION**   Ask students to create a number of subtraction models where the answer is –4. Observe whether students realize that the pairs of numbers are always 4 apart, with the minuend 4 less than the subtrahend.

MULTIPLICATION AND DIVISION OF INTEGERS

What multiplication and division sentences does the picture show?

⬇ **ONE OF THE MOST IMPORTANT** things that students must understand about calculating with integers is that the meanings remain the same as with whole numbers. Just as with whole numbers, multiplication is a way of counting the total of a number of equal groups, so 4 × (–3) could represent 4 jumps of –3 on a number line, which would get you to –12, or it could represent 4 groups of –3, which is –12. Just as with whole numbers, –12 ÷ 4 could mean that –12 is shared equally into 4 parts, so each part is –3. Just as with whole numbers, –12 ÷ (–4) could ask how many sets of –4 are in –12, and the answer is 3. Notice, however, that different meanings are used for the two division operations in order to make sense of the situation. Multiplication and division of integers is introduced in **Common Core State Standards 7.NS**.

The picture provided here is intended to emphasize the connection between multiplication and division. In this case, a student sees $2 \times (-6) = -12$ [there are two groups of -6, totaling -12], but also $-12 \div 2 = -6$ [if -12 is separated into 2 equal groups, each group holds -6] and $-12 \div (-6) = 2$ [there are 2 groups of -6 in -12].

Another way to help students understand how multiplication of integers works is to use patterns. For example, since

$$3 \times 3 = 9$$
$$3 \times 2 = 6$$
$$3 \times 1 = 3$$
$$3 \times 0 = 0,$$

it only makes sense to continue the pattern by saying that $3 \times (-1) = -3$. Or, since

$$(-3) \times 2 = -6$$
$$(-3) \times 1 = -3$$
$$(-3) \times 0 = 0,$$

it only makes sense to continue the pattern by saying that $(-3) \times (-1) = 3$.

Division can then be explained in terms of multiplication. For example, since $-3 \times -2 = +6$, then $+6 \div (-3)$ must equal -2.

? QUESTIONS to supplement the question with the picture and to include in a conversation about the picture include

- *Why would a multiplication sentence describe this picture?* [We want students to observe the two equal groups in each case.]

- *Why could you always write a division sentence if you could write a multiplication sentence?* [We want students to recognize that when a whole is divided into equal parts, there is division.]

- *Why are there two possible division sentences? How are the sentences alike and different? How are the meanings alike and different?* [We want students to realize that one division sentence asks for the size of the whole group knowing the number of smaller groups and the other for the number of smaller groups knowing the size of the whole group.]

- *Are there two possible multiplication sentences?* [We want students to consider whether the sentence $(-6) \times 2 = -12$ does or does not make sense to them here.]

◆ EXTENSION   Ask students why it might be difficult to create a picture for $12 \div (-4)$ that makes sense. This is actually quite difficult, since it makes no sense to share among -4 and there are not really groups of -4 in 12.

AREA OF A PARALLELOGRAM

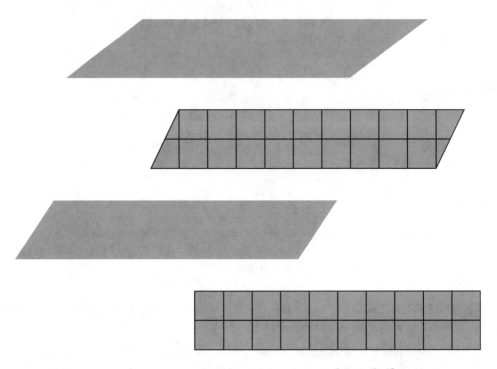

How are the areas similar? How are they different?

❯❯ **AS STUDENTS MOVE UP** through the grades, they learn to simplify measurement calculations by figuring more complex measurements using simpler ones. Initially, they work with rectangles, but soon they expand to other shapes, such as the parallelogram. The picture shown here is intended for use *prior to* the introduction of the formula for the area of a parallelogram.

It is complicated to calculate the area of a nonrectangular parallelogram since it would require the use of a grid or unit tiles. But once formulas are introduced, it is possible to calculate an area using only a length tool, a ruler. The most important idea for students to learn about the formula for the area of the parallelogram is that it is the base length and height of the parallelogram that matter, and not the "slanted" side lengths. In other words, two different parallelograms that look very different but have the same height and base length have the same area. The reason is that if one end is cut off and moved to the other end, the slants will match, no matter what they are, and the end result will be a rectangle.

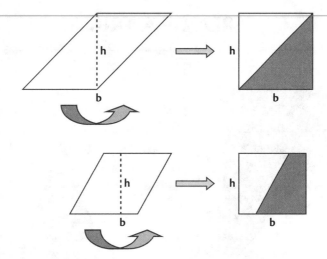

The formula for the area of a parallelogram is part of **Common Core State Standards 6.G**.

The picture of the orange shapes is intended to simplify the calculation of two areas through the use of a grid, but it also provides students opportunities to consider that parallelograms with the same area can look different. It might be desirable to have students actually create and cut out the parallelograms to see that the areas are the same.

? QUESTIONS to supplement the questions with the picture and to include in a conversation about the picture include

- *What is the same about the shapes? What is different?* [We want students to observe that all of the parallelograms and the rectangle have the same height and base length.]

- *Which shapes are easiest for you to calculate the area of? Why?* [We want students to realize that grids help us calculate areas and/or that calculating the areas of rectangles is simpler since the equal rows are more obvious.]

- *How could you decompose and then recompose the pieces to make it easier to calculate the areas of the parallelograms?* [We want students to realize that the parallelograms could be reshaped into rectangles without losing area.]

- *Why doesn't the slant of the parallelograms matter when calculating their areas?* [We want students to observe that when the parallelograms are decomposed and recomposed into rectangles, the slanting sides fit together without changing the total length of the base and thus do not affect the area of the rectangle formed.]

◆ EXTENSION   Ask students to create a variety of parallelograms that look very different but have the same area. They should realize that as long as base × height has the same value in each case, that is all that matters.

AREA OF A TRIANGLE

How are the areas of the purple triangles related to the areas of the other shapes?

❖ **NORMALLY, THE FORMULA** for the area of a triangle is introduced after the formula for the area of a parallelogram. This is because it is relatively easy to show how a right triangle or an acute triangle is half of a related rectangle, but it is harder (but not impossible) to show how an obtuse triangle is half of a related rectangle. The related rectangles all have the same height and base as the triangle.

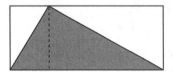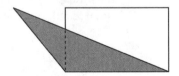

It is easy to show, however, that each triangle is half of a parallelogram with the same base and height as the triangle.

The right triangle is not shown again since the right triangle was already shown as half a parallelogram (a rectangular parallelogram). The picture shown here is intended to be used *prior to* the introduction of the formula for the area of a triangle.

Part of student learning should be recognizing the value of being able to calculate area by using just linear measures. When it comes to the triangle, specifically, the most important idea for students to learn about the formula for the area of the triangle is that it is the base length and height of the triangle that matter, and not the angle measures or all three side lengths. In other words, two triangles may look very different, but if they have the same height and same base length, they will have the same area. It is also useful for students to realize that they can multiply the base by the height and divide by two, or they can multiply the base by half the height or the height by half the base. The formula for the area of a triangle is discussed in **Common Core State Standards 6.G**.

The visual provided is intended to model the relationship between areas of triangles, rectangles, and parallelograms.

? **QUESTIONS** to supplement the question with the picture and to include in a conversation about the picture include

- *What does the picture show you about what measurements of a triangle matter when you calculate its area?* [We want students to see that it is the base and height that matter.]

- *Can every acute triangle be half of a rectangle? Half of a parallelogram?* [We want students to see that the formula does not apply to just some triangles.]

- *Is every triangle half of a parallelogram?* [We want students to realize this is true for obtuse triangles, too.]

- *What do the pictures tell you about the formula for the area of a triangle?* [We want students to see the area is half of the product of the base and the height.]

- *Why is it useful to have a formula for the area of a triangle?* [We want students to realize how much simpler it is to determine linear measures than area measures of a shape.]

- *Some people say that to build a triangle with an area of 20 square units, the base could be 4 and the height could be 10, but others say the base could be 2 and the height could be 5 since you take half when you calculate the area of a triangle. With whom do you agree? Why?* [We want students to know that the product of the base and height should be double, not half of, the area of the triangle.]

◆ **EXTENSION**   Ask students to create a parallelogram and a triangle with the same area and the same height. Ask what they notice about the base. The goal is to have students realize that the base of the triangle must be double the base of the parallelogram.

THE PYTHAGOREAN THEOREM

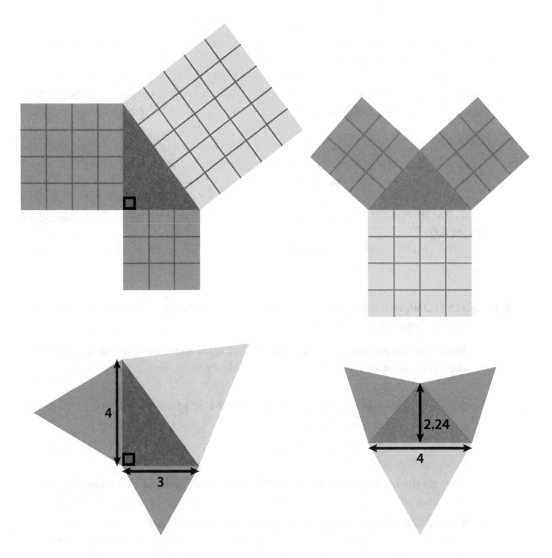

Figure out the areas of each of the colored squares and triangles. What do you notice?

THERE ARE SEVERAL critical concepts related to the Pythagorean theorem:

- There is a numerical interpretation relating the squares of the side lengths of triangles and a geometric interpretation relating the areas of squares on the sides of the triangle.

- It applies only to right triangles.
- The geometric interpretation generalizes to any mathematically similar shapes on the three sides of a right triangle, i.e., the area on the hypotenuse is the sum of the areas on the legs whenever similar shapes are drawn on all three of the original sides.

The Pythagorean theorem is important because so many concepts in geometry and measurement are built on it. The picture shown here is intended to be used *prior to* the introduction of the Pythagorean theorem, which is first addressed in **Common Core State Standards 8.G**.

The picture provided is intended to show the geometric interpretation of the theorem, as well as the extension that the area of the shape on the hypotenuse is the sum of the areas on the other two sides, regardless of the shape, as long as the shapes are mathematically similar. Students will need a hard copy on which to work unless the digital image is projected with a grid on top of the two lower pictures. If students measure on their own, they should use inch or centimeter units rather than the unit numbers in the pictures.

? QUESTIONS to supplement the question with the picture and to include in a conversation about the picture include

- *What do you notice about all of the "inside" (purple and green) triangles?* [We want students to realize that the theorem only applies to right triangles.]

- *What do you notice about the sizes of the squares on the three sides of the top purple triangle?* [We want students to notice, in the simplest situation with gridded squares, that the sum of the areas of the two smaller squares totals the area of the larger one.]

- *What do you notice about the areas of the yellow squares as compared to the areas of the pink squares for each of the top two triangles?*

- *How are the triangles on the sides of the right triangle (the bottom purple one) related?* [We want students to notice that the external triangles are all equilateral.]

- *What do you notice about the areas of the pink equilateral triangles that surround the green triangle as compared to the area of the yellow one?* [We want students to notice that the sum of the areas of the two smaller triangles (the pink ones) totals the area of the larger one (the yellow one) for the right triangle (the purple one), but not for the non-right triangle (the green one).]

◆ EXTENSION   Ask students to draw rectangles with lengths double their widths on each side of a right triangle and determine whether the areas of the two smaller rectangles still add up to equal the area of the larger one. They should realize that this is indeed the case and would still be the case if the lengths had been triple the widths, four times the widths, or half the widths. All that matters is that the shapes on the three sides are similar.

PI

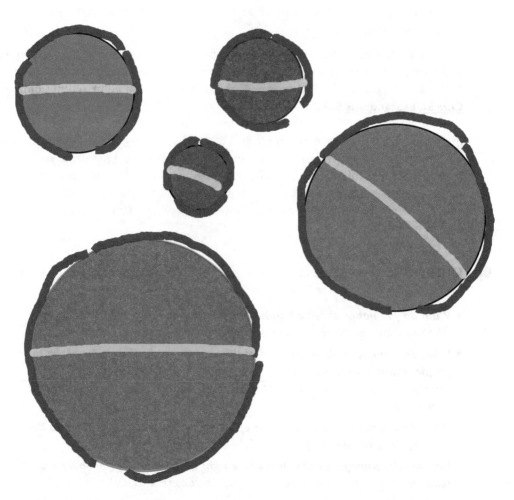

Notice that there is a yellow string across each circle and pieces of brown string around each circle. If you drew another circle and divided the circumference by the diameter, what number would you get? How do you know?

❖ **THE MOST IMPORTANT THING** we want students to understand about the number π (pi) is that it is the ratio of the circumference of any circle of any size to that circle's diameter. Although students may learn that the number is 3.14, many do not really have a good understanding that this means that it would take three strings the length of the diameter, plus a little, to wrap around the circle one time. The concept of π as the ratio of the circumference of a circle to its diameter is described in **Common Core State Standards 7.G**.

The picture provided is intended to show the notion that the circumference is slightly more than three times the size of the diameter, no matter the size of the circle. This is another way of saying that the ratio of circumference to diameter is π. It might be very useful to provide students with circular objects, scissors, and pieces of string so they can mimic what they see in the picture.

? QUESTIONS to supplement the questions with the picture and to include in a conversation about the picture include

- *Why does it make sense that if a circle has a larger diameter, it has a larger circumference?* [We want students to recognize that all measures of a circle are interrelated.]

- *What does the picture show about how long the circumference is compared with the diameter?* [We want students to relate the lengths of the wrapped strings and the yellow strings to the ratio of the circumference and diameter. There is no specific statement suggesting that the brown strings surrounding the circle are equal in length or that they are same length as the yellow string across the circle. Students are likely to speculate about this, and it either can be confirmed or a teacher can suggest that it be investigated.]

- *How many strings the length of the radius would be needed to wrap around the circle?* [We want students to recognize that since the circumference and diameter are related, and the diameter and radius are related, then the circumference and the radius are related.]

- *How much of a string the length of the circumference would fit across the diameter? Is it more or less than $\frac{1}{3}$ of it?* [We want students to know that if π is the ratio of the circumference to the diameter, then $\frac{1}{\pi}$, which is less than $\frac{1}{3}$, is the ratio of the diameter to the circumference.]

◆ EXTENSION   Ask students to draw a square around a circle, with the circle touching the square once on each side. Ask how that helps make sense of why the ratio of the circumference to the diameter is π. The objective is to have students explain that since the perimeter of the square is 4 times the diameter of the circle and the circumference of the circle definitely looks like it is just a bit less than the perimeter of the square, it makes sense that the circumference is more than 3 times the length of the diameter but less than 4 times the length.

HOW MEASURES ARE AND ARE NOT RELATED

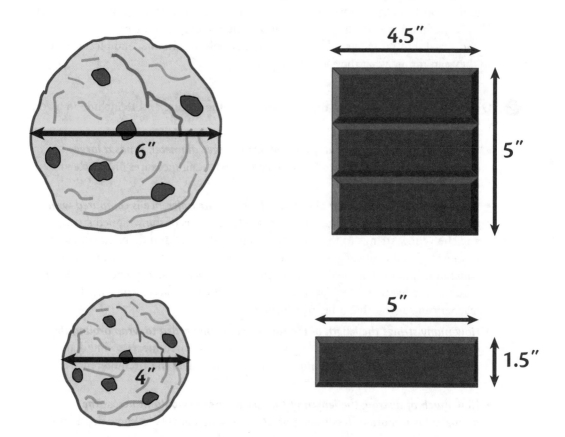

A cookie has a circumference of 10". A candy bar has a perimeter of 10". Can you be sure which has more area?

❖ **ONE OF THE MOST IMPORTANT** measurement concepts for students to learn is that sometimes measurements of a shape are related and sometimes they are not. For example, in the case of a circle, every measure is related to every other; if you know the circle's circumference, you automatically know its diameter, radius, and area. In the case of a parallelogram, however, if you know one side length, you also know one other side length, but you do not know its perimeter, area, or other side lengths. The notion that circles are special and that all of their measures are related is implicit in **Common Core State Standards 7.G**.

The picture provided portrays a circle and a rectangle with similar "perimeters" and similar areas and a circle and a rectangle with similar "perimeters" and dissimilar areas. When confronted with the question about a 10" circumference and a 10" perimeter, students have to decide with which measurement possibilities to experiment. It takes a small suspension of reality to consider the cookies and candy bars as two-dimensional, but this is not likely to be much of a hurdle in this circumstance.

(?) QUESTIONS to supplement the question with the picture and to include in a conversation about the picture include

* *Can you figure out the radius of the circles? How?* [We want students to describe how the circumference and radius measures are related.]

* *What are the circumferences and areas of the two cookies? What formulas did you use?* [We want students to describe how the radius, area, and circumference measures of a circle are related.]

* *How do the perimeters of the candy bars relate to the circumferences of the circles? How do the areas relate?* [We want students to see that a rectangle can have a perimeter similar to a circle, but its area may or may not be close to the area of the circle. There may be students who think that, in both cases in the provided picture, the areas of the candy bars are about 5 square units different from the areas of the cookies, so that in both cases, they are not close to the areas of the cookies. However, it is easy to see visually that the top candy bar's area is not much different from the top cookie's area (actually about 80% of it) but the bottom candy bar's area is much smaller than the cookie's (actually only about 60% of it).]

* *Suppose there were a third cookie with a 10" circumference and a third candy bar with a 10" perimeter? Would you be sure of the cookie's area? What about the candy bar's area?* [We want students to know that there is no uncertainty about the area of the new cookie, but there is uncertainty about the area of a candy bar with a given perimeter.]

* *Why might someone say that measurements associated with rectangles are less related to each other than measurements associated with circles?* [We want students to recognize the intrinsic relationship between all measures of a circle, but not of a rectangle.]

◆ EXTENSION   Ask students to think of other shapes where knowing one measurement ensures you know all measurements. They might think of equilateral triangles, squares, or 3-D shapes such as spheres or cubes.

MEAN

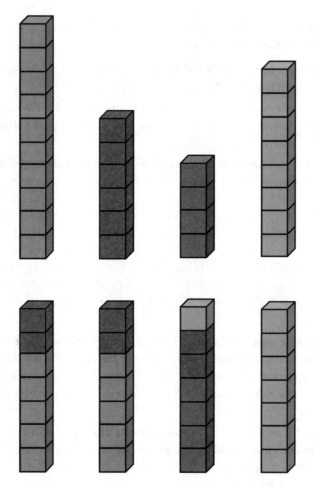

What does this picture show?
Why might this process be useful?

✦ **CALCULATING AN AVERAGE**, typically a mean, is a useful skill. Even outside of school, students will repeatedly be exposed to averages and need an understanding of what they represent. Unlike a median, which is simply the middle number when a group of numbers is ordered, the mean actually represents the share size if the total amount is shared fairly. For example, if a set of data represents the amount of money 10 different people have, the mean would tell how much each person would get if the total is shared among them evenly. The concept of mean is addressed in **Common Core State Standards 6.SP**.

The picture provided portrays a set of raw data where the values of the individual items are unequal—10, 6, 4, and 8 (or multiples thereof since each cube could represent any number)—and shows how amounts can be shifted around to create items that have equal value, 7 (or the appropriate multiple of 7) each. The intent is to help the students recognize that the mean is that equal value.

? QUESTIONS to supplement the questions with the picture and to include in a conversation about the picture include

- *What data might the cubes in the top picture represent?* [We want students to focus on the fact that data always have meaning.]

- *How are the top and bottom pictures different?* [We want students to notice the lack of equality in the first instance and the equality of values in the second instance.]

- *How would you calculate the mean of the top set of numbers?* [We want students to discuss what they already know about calculating the mean.]

- *When you divide the total of the data by 4, what are you actually doing? How does that relate to the bottom picture?* [We want students to relate the calculation of the mean to the notion of sharing.]

- *Why is it harder to describe the first set of data using just one number?* [We want students to understand that it is hard to describe both the center and spread of a set of data with a single number unless the data have been equalized, as is done when using the mean.]

◆ EXTENSION   Ask students to use linking cubes to show that there could be many sets of four pieces of data, all with the same mean. They should list those data sets. Ideally they should see that the value of any item can be increased by the same amount that the value of another item is decreased to make this work.

VARIABILITY

Tiger
200 kg

Giraffe
1600 kg

Hippo
2700 kg

Polar Bear
600 kg

Penguin
750 g

How would you describe these data about masses to someone?

STATISTICS HAS BECOME an important part of our everyday world, and students must recognize that we are often faced with data that are highly variable and yet we must use the data we have to make predictions. Students need to know that when we describe a set of data, we must have some indication of how variable those data are to make sense of them. The notion of recognizing variability in data is mentioned in **Common Core State Standards 6.SP**.

The picture shows the variability in a set of animal masses. Notice that there are both very light and very heavy masses, as well as those in between. The objective is to force students to consider whether using just an average is a good enough way to describe this collection of animal masses.

? **QUESTIONS** to supplement the question with the picture and to include in a conversation about the picture include

- *How similar are the masses of the animals? How different?* [We want students to notice how much variation there actually is.]

- *In what sort of group of animals do you think the masses would be more similar? Would they be exactly the same?* [We want students to think about how the sample examined can affect the variability of data.]

- *In what sort of group of animals do you think the masses would be even more varied? Why?*

- *What would you do to describe a typical mass for the group in the picture?* [We want students to realize that we usually use some sort of measure of central tendency to describe a typical piece of data.]

- *How would you indicate what would make a mass atypical for this group?* [We want students to realize that we usually use some measure of variation, such as range, to describe what would make data atypical.]

◆ **EXTENSION**   Ask students to think of another population where some measure would vary and discuss how they would come up with a reasonable typical measure and an indicator of what would be atypical. For example, they might consider income or education levels in different countries.

SAMPLING

What conclusion can you draw about whether most people are willing to contribute to a new community pool?

❖ **AN IMPORTANT STATISTICAL IDEA** students must grasp is the concept that sometimes we deliberately choose not to consult with every single person in a group who might be affected by a decision or whose opinion we want; instead we ask only a sample of people. Normally, we use a sample either to save costs or time or because asking everyone is actually impossible. Often we select that sample "randomly"; for example, we might assign everyone a number and use a device that generates random numbers to decide which of those people to ask. The notion of sampling is mentioned in **Common Core State Standards 7.SP**.

The picture provided shows data that might have been collected from various interviewers in answer to the question about contributing to the new community pool. Notice that some answers are positive about the contribution, but some are not. There are more people who agreed than disagreed, but we want students to go one step further and realize that the numbers alone are not necessarily enough to make a decision; they also need to find out a bit more about how the sample relates to the total population.

? QUESTIONS to supplement the question with the picture and to include in a conversation about the picture include

- *Do you feel confident that enough people were asked to make a decision?* [We want students to realize that for a community question, several hundred people is probably a decent sized sample, if the sample was random. It might not be a big enough sample to ask about a question affecting the whole country or world, however.]

- *What might you want to know about who was asked before you make your decision?* [We want students to realize that if the sample is random, we really do not need to know about the actual make-up of the sample, but otherwise, we might.]

- *What might you want to know about when and where these people were asked?* [We want students to recognize that bias can be introduced depending on where or when a question is posed.]

- *Is it possible that it might be wise to still decide "no" even though the majority said "yes"?* [We want students to consider the broad variety of factors (e.g., the amount of the financial contribution) that might go into making this type of decision based on the survey question.]

◆ EXTENSION   Ask students to think about how they would go about selecting a sample to report on people's opinions about an issue of their choice when a complete census is not feasible. For example, they might consider gathering opinions on whether army troops should go to help a country at war or whether the voting age should change.

PROBABILITY: WHAT IT MEANS

Tara's Songs

What probabilities might be related to randomly choosing a song from Tara's download library?

❖ **MANY EVENTS** in our world are somewhat random. We might have a sense that certain events are likely or unlikely, but we cannot be sure whether a specific event will or will not occur on any specific occasion. This is the premise of probability; mathematically, we can use a number (a fraction, decimal, or percent) to describe how likely something is in theory, but we still cannot be absolutely sure about what will happen on any one specific occasion. Concepts of randomness are first mentioned in **Common Core State Standards 7.SP**.

The picture provided gives a context in which to consider probability, but without the detail that might inhibit students from coming up with their own ideas. Students might consider the probabilities of genres, of particular artists, of a particular song, of songs released in a particular year, etc.

? **QUESTIONS** to supplement the question with the picture and to include in a conversation about the picture include

- *Would the number of songs in Tara's library influence any of the probabilities? Explain.* [We want students to recognize that the total sample size can influence a probability.]

- *Would the date that she started downloading songs influence any of the probabilities?* [We want students to recognize that some factors might be extraneous.]

- *In what situation would a probability be small? How small could it be without being 0?* [We want students to be aware that a small probability is one with a large denominator and small numerator.]

- *In what situation would a probability be large? How large could it be?* [We want students to realize that the maximum probability is 1.]

- *Could the same probability that a particular artist's song will be randomly selected apply in a small library as well as a large one? Explain.* [We want students to realize that probabilities, like fractions, are relative and that the same probability could occur in a small or a large sample space, depending on the number of favorable outcomes in each. For example, if a library of 8 songs included 4 rap songs and a library of 800 songs included 400 rap songs, the probability of selecting a rap song is $\frac{1}{2}$ in each.]

◆ **EXTENSION**   Ask students to think of a situation in which a probability for something real might be $\frac{3}{4}$. They might stick with music libraries, but that is not necessary. Encourage students to avoid dice games and spinners for their examples and think about a probability situation that happens in everyday life, for example, the probability that Mom will shop on Tuesday or the probability that dinner will be spaghetti.

UNPREDICTABILITY

HEADS	TAILS
卌 II	

What will happen next? How sure are you?

⟱ **ONE OF THE MOST COMMON** misconceptions people have about probability is that they can predict a particular event's outcome based on previous outcomes. For example, if a woman has had 3 girls, she might believe she is likely to have a boy next. She would be using the notion that the probability for each gender is $\frac{1}{2}$ over the long term in an attempt to predict a specific event; this is not possible. Another common misconception is that outcomes of random experiments follow a pattern; for example, many students believe that if you roll a die and get even, even, odd, odd, that the next result will have to be even to keep up the pattern. The notion that events are independent and that specific instances cannot be predicted is part of **Common Core State Standards 7.SP**.

The picture provided presents an interesting dilemma. Many students will think that the coin must be rigged and so there will only be heads. Other students will think that the result will have to be tails next because heads has had too many turns. But some students will realize that you just cannot predict; each event is independent.

❓ **QUESTIONS** to supplement the questions with the picture and to include in a conversation about the picture include

- *How often do you think you would flip 7 heads before you get a tail?* [We want students to realize how unlikely, but still possible, this situation is.]

- *What is the expected probability of landing a head when you flip a coin? Why?* [We want to establish what the theoretical probability is, in this case, a probability of 1 out of 2.]

- *If you flip a coin 10 times, how many heads would you expect to get?* [We want to see if students realize that a safer answer is between 4 and 6 (or even between 3 and 7) rather than simply 5.]

- *Could all of those heads have come in a row or is that impossible?* [We want students to realize that you cannot predict the sequence of outcomes.]

- *What do you think would come next if you had flipped 3 heads, then a tail, and then another 3 heads?* [We want students to realize that it does not matter how much outcomes look like they follow a pattern; if the events are random, there is no pattern.]

◆❯ **EXTENSION**   Ask students to consider a situation in which they would be fairly certain that an even number would be selected, but not completely certain. For example, students might suggest choosing a number off of the multiplication table. Have them discuss why an even number is more likely (in this case because $\frac{3}{4}$ of the numbers are even), but not certain (in this case because $\frac{1}{4}$ of the numbers are odd).

ROTATIONS, REFLECTIONS, AND TRANSLATIONS

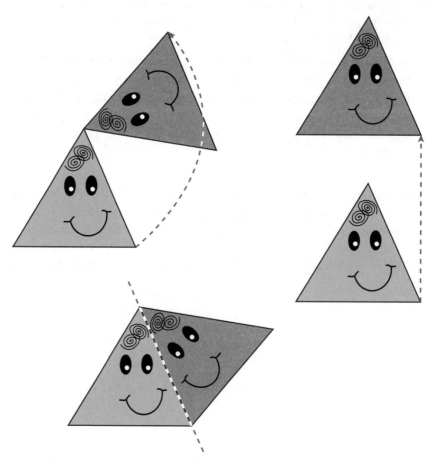

Which points on the original triangles do not move at all?
Which move pretty far?

❖ **STUDENTS LEARN** about rotations, reflections, and translations as they study transformations that preserve congruence of shapes. Although many students can distinguish among the three transformations, they sometimes struggle to articulate what the differences are. One way to think about how the transformations differ is to think about how individual points on shapes move. When using a translation, all points move. When using a reflection, all points except those on the reflection line move; points farther from the reflection line move more. When using a rotation, only one point, the center of rotation, does not move. Attention to the transformations is addressed in **Common Core State Standards 8.G**.

Each pair of triangles models one transformation. The original triangles can be considered to be the pink ones or the purple ones, whichever the student wishes. A diagonal reflection was used in the reflection picture because so many students are comfortable only with vertical and horizontal reflections; this example will give them experience with a new type.

? **QUESTIONS** to supplement the questions with the picture and to include in a conversation about the picture include

- *How did each point move in the top right picture (the translation)? What if the translation had moved the original shape to the right as well as vertically?* [We want students to recognize that any translation moves all points the same amount and direction.]

- *In the top left picture, if the triangle had been turned further, would there still be a point that didn't move? Why?* [We want students to recognize that the center of rotation never moves, regardless of the amount of the rotation.]

- *In the bottom picture, why did the bottom left corner point of the pink triangle move farther than points near the reflection line?* [We want students to realize that the distance a point moves as a result of a reflection relates to its distance from the reflection line.]

- *Is there always more than one point that doesn't move when performing a reflection?* [We want students to realize that all points on the reflection line stay fixed.]

◆ **EXTENSION**   Ask students to draw pictures of a translation, a reflection, and a rotation of a rectangle such that the bottom left corner moves a little for the translation, a little less for the reflection and a lot for the rotation. To accomplish this, they might translate, for example, 4 inches left and 2 inches down, reflect ensuring that the bottom left corner of the rectangle is fairly close to the reflection line, and rotate by placing the center of rotation at the top right corner.

SCALE DRAWINGS

Which are scale drawings? How do you know?

❖ **BEING ABLE TO CREATE** a scale drawing is a practical life skill. It is also useful in geometry in studying the concept of similar shapes. Students learn that although the size of a shape changes in a scale drawing, angle measures and proportional relationships do not. Scale drawing is addressed in **Common Core State Standards 7.G**.

The picture focuses students on the notion that scaling can reduce or increase the size of an object and that the increase or decrease can be any amount; it need not be an integer multiple. The picture also ensures that students realize that all angles must remain the same and all proportions in the original object must be preserved. Even slight variation means that the drawing is not a scale drawing.

❓ QUESTIONS to supplement the questions with the picture and to include in a conversation about the picture include

- *The owl in the center is the original. What do you think the scale ratio is for the smallest owl?* [We want students to recognize what the scale factor does.]

- *Which owl do you think is not a scaled up or down version of the original owl? Why?* [We want students to recognize that no features can be "off" in a scaled version. Note that the wings of the tallest owl are not quite right.]

- *What do you think the scale ratio is for the larger correct scale version of the owl?* [We want students to recognize that we compare linear dimensions, not area, to determine a scale factor.]

- *If the scale factor for the smaller version is 0.8, what would be the scale factor to enlarge the smaller version to the original size?* [We want students to realize that if A is a scale image of B, the reverse is also true; the scale factors are multiplicative reciprocals. In this new case, the scale factor would be 1.25.]

◆ EXTENSION   Ask students to take an interesting 2-D object and create a scale drawing with a particular scale factor. Encourage students to use decimal ratios rather than whole number ratios if they can. Then ask them to describe the scale factor going from the new picture to the old one. Finally, ask them to make another drawing that is almost, but not quite, a scale drawing.

DILATATIONS

Sara is tracing the picture of the dog.
How is the dog her pencil is creating different
from the dog she is tracing? Why?

 MUCH LIKE REFLECTIONS, rotations, and translations, dilatations are also transformations. However, a dilatation not only changes the position of a shape, but also its size. Performing a dilatation results in a shape similar to the original one. Dilatations are addressed in **Common Core State Standards 8.G**.

Dilatations can be performed by choosing a dilatation center, measuring distances to various points of the original shape and extending or shrinking those distances by a given dilatation factor (essentially a scale factor). If a shape has no identifiable vertices (e.g., a circle), then a student could choose random points to use, but there must be enough points that the student can be confident about what happens to the points in between.

The picture provided presents an interesting variation of a doubling dilatation where, instead of using a ruler and measuring, the student uses rubber bands. The dilatation with rubber bands is a bit less exact, but much quicker. The student must choose a dilatation center far enough from what he (or she) is tracing that he has to stretch the rubber bands to reach it. He places the knot of the rubber bands on what is being traced, stretches the rubber bands uniformly, and places a pencil at the end of the second rubber band to follow along as the original is being traced. The dilated image will be created. The distance between where the rubber band chain is held down and the knot connecting the two rubber bands represents the original distance to the dilatation center.

QUESTIONS to supplement the questions with the picture and to include in a conversation about the picture include

- *Why do you think the pencil is creating an object that is bigger than the original?* [We want students to realize that Sara is actually creating a dilatation with a scale factor of 2.]
- *What do you think would have happened if there had been three rubber bands instead, with the pencil at the end of the third rubber band?* [We want students to recognize how the physical arrangement affects the scale factor.]
- *Why would it be harder to do a dilatation with a factor of 1.5 using this strategy?*
- *How is the picture like what would result if you doubled the length and width of a rectangle from the top right corner and compared it to the original rectangle?* [We want students to see that this is like using the top right vertex as a dilatation center.]
- *What geometry term could you use to describe the original and final shapes?* [We want students to relate dilatations to similarity.]
- *Do you think the area of the shape will also double?* [We want students to realize that dilatations change the area measures differently than the linear measures.]

EXTENSION   Ask students to test out the rubber band dilatation strategy or, if they prefer, they can perform a dilatation using dynamic geometry software such as Geometer's Sketchpad.

ANGLES WITH PARALLEL LINES

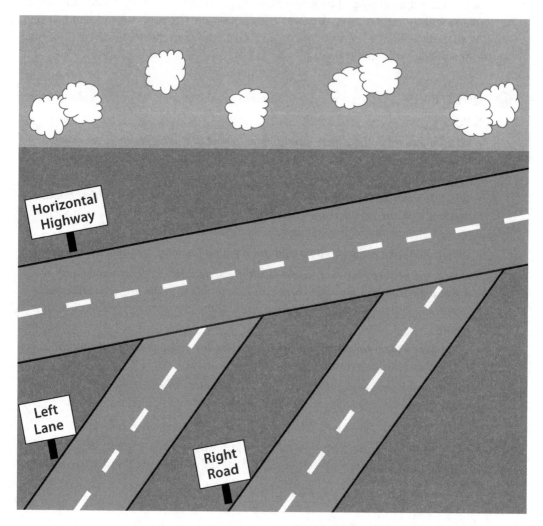

Horizontal
Highway

Left
Lane

Right
Road

How can you be sure that Left Lane and
Right Road are parallel?

WE TELL STUDENTS that two lines are parallel if they never meet; the problem, though, is that we cannot test that definition—how do we know the lines do not meet miles and miles away? There are other more indirect ways to test for parallelism, and considering angle sizes when lines are cut by a transversal is one of those ways. If two lines are parallel, the angles formed when they are cut by a third line are either equal or supplementary in particular ways; if the lines are not parallel, this would not be the case. Therefore, angle measurement is one way to test for parallelism. Properties of angles formed when parallel lines are cut by a transversal are addressed in **Common Core State Standards 8.G**.

The question with the picture asks students to consider whether two roads are parallel. Most students will say they are sure because the roads look parallel. It is up to the teacher to suggest that looks can be deceiving and to ask students to consider ways to be sure. One way is to create a perpendicular to one of the lines to see if that new line is also perpendicular to the supposedly parallel line. Another way is to use angle measures.

? QUESTIONS to supplement the question with the picture and to include in a conversation about the picture include

- *How do you know that Horizontal Highway is not perpendicular to either of the other roads?* [We want to make sure students are familiar with the concept of perpendicularity.]

- *Would a road perpendicular to Left Lane also be perpendicular to Right Road?* [We want students to realize that a common perpendicular is one way to test for parallelism.]

- *What do you know about the angle measures in the picture?* [We want students to realize which angles are equal and which are supplementary if the lines are parallel.]

- *What would you know if the angles where Horizontal Highway meets Left Lane and Right Road were not equal?* [We want students to know that if lines are not parallel, corresponding angles are not equal.]

- *How else could you test for parallelism?* [We want students to consider other possible tests, for example, measuring the distance between the lines at various points to see if the distances remain equal.]

- *Why is it useful to have strategies other than not meeting anywhere to test for parallelism?* [We want students to realize that we need a way to test for parallelism that does not depend on something that happens "forever."]

◆ EXTENSION   Ask students what they think the best way to test for parallelism is. Some students might focus on common perpendicularity, some on angle measures of corresponding angles, and others on a common distance apart. The important part is that students justify their choice.

EQUIVALENT EXPRESSIONS

$$x + (-x)$$
is a way to represent 0

$$1 + (-1)$$
is a way to represent 0

 ### is a way to represent x

 ### is a way to represent 1

What are some different ways to represent $3x + 2$?

◈ **AN IMPORTANT PART** of algebraic thinking involves renaming one expression as another. For example, we rename $3x + 2x$ as $5x$ or we rename $x^2 + 2x + 1$ as $(x + 1)^2$. Students should think of these alternate names as equivalent expressions, just as we often use equivalent fractions to simplify our number thinking. The renaming can involve alternate visual representations, such as algebra tiles, or can involve numerical or algebraic computations. For example, adding 0 is always a way to rename a number or expression, so another name for $-x$ is $-x + 4 - 4$ or $2x + (-2x) + (-x) = 2x - 3x$. Simplifying and renaming algebraic expressions is part of **Common Core State Standards 6.EE**.

The picture provided offers some material upon which students can draw to represent (rename or model) $x + 1$. They might add sets of $x + (-x)$ or sets of $1 + (-1)$, or they might use geometric models. They might also think of multiplying by some form of 1, such as $2 \div 2$ or $4 \div 4$ and express $x + 1$ as $(4x + 4) \div 4$ or using the commutative principle for addition and write $1 + x$.

? QUESTIONS to supplement the question with the picture and to include in a conversation about the picture include

- *Why are 3 + 2, 8 − 3, and 5 + 0 equivalent expressions for the number 5?* [We want students to notice that an equivalent expression is simply one with the same "result" when we are dealing with a number.]

- *What is another equivalent expression for 5?* [We want students to generate equivalent expressions for numbers to prepare them for the same task with algebraic expressions.]

- *Why can you always add zeroes to get an equivalent expression?* [We want students to know that there are some guaranteed strategies for creating equivalent expressions.]

- *Why can you always multiply by 1 to get an equivalent expression?*

- *What are other strategies for equivalence you can always use?* [We want students to generate their own strategies to develop equivalent expressions.]

◆◆ EXTENSION   Ask students to choose an algebraic expression and describe a situation where the equivalent expression looks more complicated and another where it looks less complicated. For example, they might choose $2x + 5x + 3 - 2$ and write it first as $2x + 5x - 8x + 6x + 2x + 3 - 2 - 4 + 4$ and then write it as $7x + 1$.

EQUATION AS A BALANCE

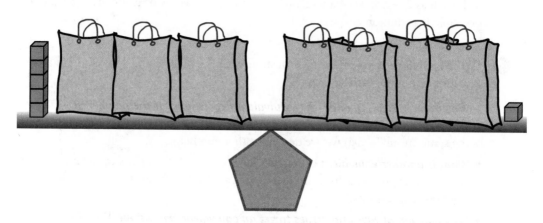

How can thinking about this balance help you solve the equation $3x + 5 = 4x + 1$?

THERE IS A FAIR BIT of research that indicates the difficulties many students have in solving equations because they interpret the equal sign as a "get the number on the other side" symbol. For example, these students solve $4 + x = 8 + 7$ by saying that $x = 4$ since $4 + 4 = 8$, the first number they see after the equals sign. There is a lot of evidence that thinking about an equation as a balance is a valuable metaphor for students. The idea is that the two sides of the balance represent equivalent amounts. Treating the equation as a balance helps a student realize he or she can add to both sides, subtract from both sides, etc., without disturbing the balance. Solving an equation using a balance model is a tool for dealing with **Common Core State Standards 6.EE**.

The picture specifically addresses an equation with a variable on both sides. Students need to realize that they must place the same number of cubes in each bag in such a way that the two sides balance to interpret the situation. They must imagine, though, that the bags are so light that their weight has no effect. For some students, it might be necessary to scaffold this idea by showing a balance with unknowns (the bags) on only one side. For example, a balance might have two bags and 7 cubes on one side and 13 cubes on the other side.

QUESTIONS to supplement the question with the picture and to include in a conversation about the picture include

- *If you thought of each bag as holding x cubes, what amounts would be on the two sides of the balance?* [We want students to relate the equation to the model.]

- *What would happen if you put 2 cubes in each bag?* [We want students to consider the effect of substituting particular values for x. They need to consider whether there is a balance or (if not) which side is heavier.]

- *What would happen if you put 6 cubes in each bag?*

- *How do you know that the number of cubes in each bag must be between 2 and 6?* [We want students to realize that if one side is heavier with one value and the other side is heavier with the other value, the solution is in between.]

- *Why might you take 3 bags off each side of the balance?* [We want students to consider ways to simplify the equation without changing the solution.]

- *How can you figure out the solution without just trying numbers?* [We want students to recognize the potential of simplifying the equation so that one bag is balanced by a set of cubes.]

◆▶ **EXTENSION**   Ask students to draw a balance to model several other equations with variables on both sides and use the balance to help them solve those equations. Most students will be more successful if they use only positive coefficients and constants (e.g., $3x + 1 = 2x + 8$), although it would be interesting for some students to try to use negative coefficients (e.g., $3x - 1 = 2x + 8$).

DIFFERENT TYPES OF EQUATIONS

How are the equations for the two balances different?

◈ **STUDENTS MEET** three different types of equations in their math experiences. One type has one or a limited number of solutions; the variable is called an unknown. An example is $3x + 4 = 10$, where $x = 2$ is the only possible solution. Another type of equation is one relating two variables, for example, $P = 4s$, relating the perimeter and side length of a square; it has many pairs of solutions. For example, if $s = 1$ and $P = 4$, we have one solution, and if $s = 3$ and $P = 12$, we have another solution. A third type of equation is one where each side of the equation is an equivalent expression for the other side, for example, $2x + 3 = 2x + 2 + 1$. Recognizing the meaning of equations with variables is first mentioned in **<u>Common Core State Standards 6.EE</u>**.

The picture provided specifically addresses two of these types of equations, one with an unknown value and one where the two sides of the equation are equivalent expressions.

❓ QUESTIONS to supplement the question with the picture and to include in a conversation about the picture include

- *What equation matches each pan balance?* [We want students to relate the physical representation to algebraic equations.]
- *What would happen if you put 2 cubes in each x bag for the first balance? For the second balance?* [We want students to consider the effect of substituting particular values for *x* in each type of equation.]
- *What if you put 4 cubes in each bag?*
- *How do you know you can't make the first balance work if you put more than 4 cubes in the x bags?* [We want students to consider why the first equation has no other solutions.]
- *How do you know you can put any number of cubes in the x bags for the second balance?* [We want students to recognize that the second equation has an infinite number of solutions.]
- *Which equation tells you that two expressions are equivalent? Which doesn't?* [We want students to recognize that if an equation equates two equivalent expressions, it will have an infinite number of solutions, but that other equations are valid only for limited values.]

◆ EXTENSION Ask students to consider the equation $A = s \times s$, which describes the area of a square. Ask which type of equation represented in the picture they think it is most like and why. Some students will argue it is not like either one since there are two variables, but you can still push for them to make a choice. Most students will suggest it is more like the bottom equation since there are many possible solutions. It is different, of course, because there are values for *s* and *A* for the new equation that do not work, but all values of *x* solve the bottom equation on the page.

WHAT IS LINEAR?

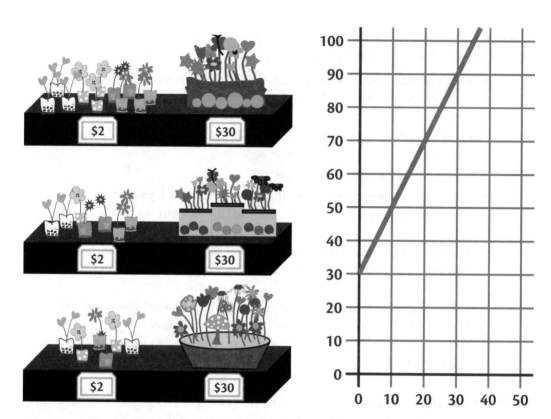

The graph tells how much someone might spend if he or she buys a number of $2 plants and a $30 planter. Where on the graph would one find the information from the three different pictures? Why is the graph a line?

⋙ **THE CONCEPT OF LINEARITY** is very important in mathematics as well as in describing many everyday phenomena. Students meet the concept of linearity in several ways; they might see a line graphed, they might observe a table of values with a constant increase, or they might encounter an equation relating y and x. What is consistent about all of these situations is that for a given change of one variable, the other variable changes the same amount. For example, if an increase of one variable from 2 to 4 results in a particular change in the second variable, then an increase of the first variable from 90 to 92 results in a change in the second variable that is exactly the same as the first change in the second variable. The concept of linearity is addressed in **Common Core State Standards 7.RP** and **8.EE**.

The picture specifically addresses two representations of linearity—a graph and a real-life situation. The focus is on observing the constancy of the increase in one variable for a constant increase in the other.

❓ QUESTIONS to supplement the questions with the picture and to include in a conversation about the picture include

- *How could you predict the cost of a purchase of one $30 item and a number of $2 items?* [We want students to build the connection between this situation and the ones in the picture by using the number of $2 items purchased as the *x*-value and looking at the line for the corresponding *y*-value.]

- *If Jane bought three more $2 items than Sarah, how much more would Jane pay? Would it depend on how many Sarah bought?* [We want students to recognize that what makes linear situations special is that a particular change in one variable leads to a particular change in the other variable, no matter the original values of the variables.]

- *What table of values would describe the situation in the picture?* [We want students to recognize other representations of the relationship using a table where the *y*-values increase by 2 when the *x*-values increase by 1 and where the *y*-value for $x = 0$ is 30.]

- *Why might the equation of the line be* y = 30 + 2x, *if x tells how many $2 plants are purchased?* [We want students to understand that this is true because the price is always at least $30 if the large planter is purchased and the additional cost is $2 per separate plant purchased.]

- *Suppose x increases by 2 in the line represented by the equation* y = 30 + 2x. *How does y change? Does it depend on the value of* x? [We want students to use either numerical or algebraic methods to see that *y* would have to increase by 2×2 when *x* increases by 2 because the equation is linear.]

- *Why might the situation described by buying many of the individual plants along with one large planter be called a linear situation?* [We want students to explore the term "linear."]

◆ EXTENSION   Ask students to describe a different linear situation, create a graph and table of values that go with it, and prove that the situation is linear. For example, the student might count heartbeats per minute or might describe a cell phone plan with a fixed cost and per minute charges.

ROLE OF THE SLOPE IN THE EQUATION OF A LINE

x	y
0	2
1	5
2	8
3	11
4	14

x	y
0	3
1	5
2	7
3	9
4	11

$y = 3x + 2$

$y = 2x + 3$

x	y
0	2
1	8
2	14
3	20
4	26

x	y
0	6
1	8
2	10
3	12
4	14

$y = 6x + 2$

$y = 2x + 6$

How do the numbers in the tables show up in each of the graphs? How do the numbers in each of the equations show up in the tables?

◈ **AS STUDENTS LEARN** to use graphs of lines to solve problems, they come to understand that it is the coefficient of the *x* variable that describes the steepness, or slope, of a line, not the constant term. But we also want students to relate that number in the equation to the first differences (i.e., the differences between consecutive *y*-values) in a table of values. This material is best addressed *prior to* any direct teaching of the fact that *m* represents the slope in the equation $y = mx + b$. Recognizing the slope in the equation of a line is addressed in **Common Core State Standards 8.EE**.

The picture depicts the tables of values and graphs for two sets of lines where the values of the slope and intercept are interchanged. This will help students see the different roles that these two values play in terms of the graph and in terms of the table of values.

❓ QUESTIONS to supplement the question with the picture and to include in a conversation about the picture include

- *How can you tell which table of values goes with which graph in each case?* [We want students to relate the way the *y* values in a table increase to the slope of the graph.]

- *Which graph in each pair is steepest? How is that reflected in the table of values?* [We want students to realize that the more quickly the *y*-values in a table change, the steeper the slope.]

- *What does the m in y = mx + b tell you about the line? What does the b tell you?* [We want students to observe that *m* is the slope and *b* is the *y*-intercept.]

- *Suppose you want a graph to go up even more quickly than these. What might the equation be? What would the table of values look like?* [We want students to generalize from these examples to consider a different case.]

◈ EXTENSION   Ask students to consider the equations $y = -3x - 2$ and $y = -2x - 3$ to see if the roles of *m* and *b* change when values are negative.

SYSTEMS OF EQUATIONS

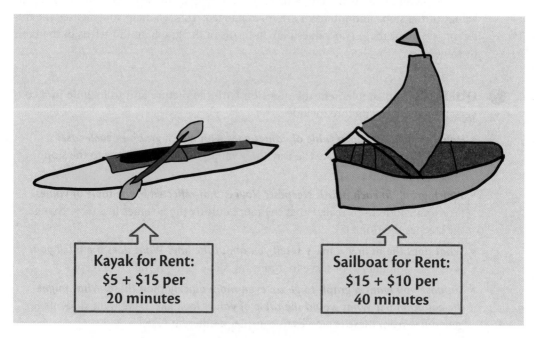

Kayak for Rent:
$5 + $15 per
20 minutes

Sailboat for Rent:
$15 + $10 per
40 minutes

When the two different boat rentals are compared, is there a number of minutes for which they cost the same amount?

THERE ARE OFTEN INSTANCES in mathematics when we are comparing two different situations. For example, in elementary school, students might compare the results of multiplying two numbers to adding them; students learn that with whole numbers, multiplication usually (but not always) yields a greater result, but with proper fractions, the opposite usually occurs. As students go into higher grades, the comparisons are often between algebraic situations, and this is often more complex.

One of the first situations students study is the comparison of two linear equations, to see for which values one is greater and for which values the other is greater; there are many practical situations to which this might apply. Students learn that if the graphs of the two lines intersect, there is one and only one value of x where the results are equal, and one relationship gives a result that is greater than the result of the other for all x-values greater than the x-value at the intersection point and less for all other x-values. Sometimes, however, the lines are parallel; in that case, the y-values for one line are always greater than the corresponding y-values for the other line. The concept of systems of linear equations is addressed in **Common Core State Standards 8.EE**.

The picture provided here suggests one of the common situations in which comparisons of linear relationships might occur. In this particular case, responses might vary. Some students will assume that even if a person goes out for less than 20 minutes in the kayak or less than 40 minutes in the sailboat, the person will still have to pay the full 20-minute or 40-minute cost. Others will assume that the costs are prorated. This difference of opinion can stimulate an interesting discussion of what the consequences would be.

? **QUESTIONS** to supplement the question with the picture and to include in a conversation about the picture include

- *Which plan is better if you go out for only 10 minutes?* [We want students to substitute values to get a feel for the functions provided.]

- *Which plan is better if you go out for 40 minutes?*

- *Why does it make sense that the sailboat will be cheaper if you go out for longer times?* [We want students to notice that the variable cost has the most impact in the long term.]

- *If you drew graphs of these costs in which the values on the x-axis represented the minutes out and the values on the y-axis represented the cost, what would you notice about the graphs? Why does that make sense?* [We want students who prorate the costs to relate the equal costs to the intersection point of two lines on a graph and realize that, if two lines cross, the differences increase the farther away from that intersection point you go.]

- *Why, for students who prorate the costs, would there never be more than one number of minutes for which the plans cost the same?* [We want students to realize that these are lines and that lines are either parallel or they cross only at one point.]

- *When might one plan always be costlier than another?* [We want students to realize that using the same variable costs, but different initial costs, ensures that one plan is always costlier.]

- *How would that show up in the graph?* [We want students to relate the situation to parallel lines.]

◆ **EXTENSION**   Ask students to create two canoe renting plans that cost exactly the same when the number of minutes is 100 minutes and only 100 minutes. An example might be a prorated plan that is $20 + $10 per 20 minutes and $40 + $6 per 20 minutes.

FUNCTION RULES

Do you think the wizard can do this?
Would he be able to give the start number if
the rule on the machine were different?

❖ **THE NOTION OF FUNCTIONS** informally starts in very early grades when students use rules like "add 3" or "double the number" to use an input number to get a particular output number. The notion becomes formalized later, with particular types of notation added, and is fundamental to much of secondary school mathematics learning. The basic concept is that if a function (often a rule expressed algebraically, although it could be expressed verbally) is well defined, as soon as you provide an input, a single consistent output is the result. The concept of functions is addressed in **Common Core State Standards 8.F**.

The picture shows the potential for using what are later called inverse functions to "read people's minds." For example, if you know that the function says "double a number" and you know the result is 8, you can apply the function in reverse to tell someone that the number they started with was 4, even if they did not tell you this number.

❓ QUESTIONS to supplement the question with the picture and to include in a conversation about the picture include

- *Suppose the person started with 3. What would the wizard give as his answer?* [We want to ensure that students can apply a simple function rule.]

- *What would the wizard say if the answer were 50? How do you know?* [We want students to work backward in a particular case and explain their thinking. Since the doubled sum was 50, the first sum was 25. But that came from adding 5 to a doubled number, so the original number must have been 10.]

- *What would the wizard say if the answer were 45? How do you know?* [We want students to recognize that the starting number does not have to be a whole number. In this case, it would be 8.75.]

- *How does the wizard figure out his answer? Why does that make sense?* [We want students to articulate the inverse function and explain their thinking or else recognize that they were essentially solving the equation $2(2x + 5) = n$ for a given n.]

- *Suppose the rule were "double your number, subtract 5, and then double your answer." Do you think the wizard could still figure out the start number from the answer? Explain.* [We want students to recognize that other functions work in a similar way.]

- *Why might it be harder for the wizard if the rule had been "square your number"?* [We want students to explore the idea that the opposites (inverses) of functions need not be functions. It would not be clear whether to take the positive or negative square root.]

◆ EXTENSION Ask students to create their own magic tricks of this sort for other students to figure out.

APPENDIX

Connections Between Topics and Common Core State Standards

Number and Operations—Fractions

The Number System

Operations and Algebraic Thinking

Ratios and Proportional Relationships

Statistics and Probability

References

Adams, R. D., & Victor, M. (1993). *Principles of neurology* (5th ed.). New York: McGraw-Hill.

Bruce, C. D. (2007). *Student interaction in the math classroom: Stealing ideas or building understanding.* Toronto: Ministry of Education, the Literacy and Numeracy Secretariat.

Common Core State Standards for Mathematics. (2010). Available at http://www.corestandards.org/assets/CCSSI_Math%20Standards.pdf

Dougherty, B., Flores, A., Louis, E., Sophian, C., & Zbiek, R. (2010). *Developing essential understanding of number and numeration for teaching mathematics in preK–2.* Reston, VA: National Council of Teachers of Mathematics.

Hufferd-Ackles, K., Fuson, K. C., & Sherin, M. G. (2004). Describing levels and components of a math-talk learning community. *Journal of Research in Mathematics Education, 35,* 81–116.

Lampert, M., & Cobb, P. (2003). Communication and language. In J. Kilpatrick, W. G. Martin, & D. Schifter (Eds.), *A research companion to* Principles and Standards for School Mathematics (pp. 237–249). Reston, VA: National Council of Teachers of Mathematics.

Murphy, S. (2007). *Visual learning in elementary mathematics.* Pearson Education. Available at http://assets.pearsonschool.com/asset_mgr/legacy/200748/enVision_Murphy-monograph_2523_1.pdf

National Council of Teachers of Mathematics. (2000). *Principles and standards for school mathematics.* Reston, VA: Author.

National Council of Teachers of Mathematics. (2006). *Curriculum focal points for prekindergarten through grade 8.* Reston, VA: Author.

Nelsen, R. B. (2000). *Proofs without words II: More exercises in visual thinking.* Washington, DC: The Mathematics Association of America.

Rowan, T., & Bourne, B. (1994). *Thinking like mathematicians: Putting the K–4 NCTM standards into practice.* Portsmouth, NH: Heinemann.

Sadoski, M., & Paivio, A. (2001). *Imagery and text: A dual coding theory of reading and writing.* Mahwah, NJ: Lawrence Erlbaum Associates.

Sullivan, P., & Clarke, D. (1992). Problem solving with conventional mathematics content: Responses of pupils to open mathematical tasks. *Mathematics Education Research Journal, 4,* 42–60.

Tufte, E. R. (2001). *The visual display of quantitative information.* Cheshire, CN: Graphics Press.

Index

About the Authors

MARIAN SMALL is the former Dean of Education at the University of New Brunswick. She speaks regularly about differentiating instruction and asking better questions in K–12 mathematics.

She has been an author on many mathematics text series at both the elementary and the secondary levels. She has served on the author team for the National Council of Teachers of Mathematics (NCTM) Navigation series (pre-K–2), as the NCTM representative on the Mathcounts question writing committee for middle-school mathematics competitions throughout the United States, and as a member of the editorial panel for the NCTM 2011 yearbook on motivation and disposition.

Dr. Small is probably best known for her books *Good Questions: Great Ways to Differentiate Mathematics Instruction* and *More Good Questions: Great Ways to Differentiate Secondary Mathematics Instruction* (with Amy Lin). She has recently completed the second edition of a text for university pre-service teachers and practicing teachers, *Making Math Meaningful to Canadian Students: K–8*, as well as the professional resources *Big Ideas from Dr. Small: Grades 4–8*; *Big Ideas from Dr. Small: Grades K–3*; and *Leaps and Bounds toward Math Understanding: Grades 3–4, Grades 5–6*, and *Grades 7–8*, all published by Nelson Education Ltd.

She led the research resulting in the creation of maps describing student mathematical development in each of the five NCTM mathematical strands for the K–8 levels and has created the associated professional development program, PRIME.

AMY LIN's background in the sciences and the arts helps explain why her passion in mathematics education is to develop both the logical and the creative aspects of the subject. She is often asked to speak on mathematics teaching and learning and is an author of a number of mathematics resources for students and teachers at both the elementary and the secondary levels.

Amy has won awards for teaching and leadership and has worked as a department head, a district consultant, and a government consultant and researcher. She has initiated and successfully led many professional development projects in school districts. She has significant expertise with differentiated instruction for student success and with the use of technology supports for students.